MW01222658

Meet My Shadow

I'm twenty-three. I'm an alcoholic. Nobody knows. I live a lie. I need sobriety. I'm too ashamed. I'm closing in on rock bottom. I'm terrified.

Lisa,
It was a pleasure
to meet you.
Call me anytime.

LUKE TOUGAS

iUniverse, Inc.
New York Bloomington

iUniverse books may be ordered through booksellers or by contacting:

iUniverse
1663 Liberty Drive
Bloomington, IN 47403
www.iuniverse.com
1-800-Authors (1-800-288-4677)

Because of the dynamic nature of the Internet, any Web addresses or links contained in this book may have changed since publication and may no longer be valid. The views expressed in this work are solely those of the author and do not necessarily reflect the views of the publisher, and the publisher hereby disclaims any responsibility for them.

ISBN: 978-1-4502-1278-6 (sc)
ISBN: 978-1-4502-1280-9 (hc)
ISBN: 978-1-4502-1279-3 (ebook)

Printed in the United States of America

iUniverse rev. date: 06/18/2010

The names and other identifying details of some characters have been changed to protect individual privacy and anonymity.

I dedicate this book to my godfather who was never given that second chance.

Rest in peace, Uncle Gary.

Scars have the strange power to remind us that our past is real. The events that cause them can never be forgotten.

Cormac McCarthy, *All the Pretty Horses*

Introduction

I park Jimmy next to an old Buick. The rain picks up. I walk toward the building. My heart pounds. I try one door. It's locked. Raindrops drip off my hair onto my face. I try the second door. It's locked. I hope it's cancelled. I walk to a third door. It opens. A wise-looking old man turns his head. He looks confused. Within seconds, he knows. He sees my broken spirit.

"Hey, son. Are you here for the AA meeting?"

I nod. I have no words hearing that question for the first time.

"It's at the end of the hall to your left."

I smile.

He smiles back.

The building is empty. I feel hollow. I feel sick. I follow my footsteps. I walk into an old classroom. There are only old people. I want to make sure I'm in the right place. I don't want to mention AA. I'm embarrassed. I'm ashamed. I walk up to a lady in her mid-forties. She looks gentle. This can't be AA. These people look happy.

"Is this the place?" I softly mumble.

"What place?" I could be a punk. It's anonymous. We stare into each other's eyes.

"AA?"

"Yes. Welcome. What's your name?"

"Luke." We shake hands.

"Hi, Luke, I'm Jane. Is this your first meeting?" She sees the shattered pieces.

"Yes, it is."

"Oh, well, let's get you started. Come here for a second."

I follow Jane to the front of the class. She goes into a closet. She comes out with a big book.

"Here you go, Luke; don't feel pressure to read any of this, but when you get some time or feel like drinking, read *Alcoholics Anonymous*. It might help you out."

"Great. How much do I owe you?"

"It's on us." Jane smiles.

I feel welcomed.

"You are very kind."

"It's our pleasure. If you want to take a seat, we'll get started."

"Thank you."

I sit in the back corner. I listen. I sense doubt. They ask if new members want to identify themselves. I sit passively. When it's over, I'm the first one out. I speed-walk to Jimmy. I crank my tunes. I bang my head against the steering wheel. "Fuck!" I'm not like these people. I know I have a problem, but I can't be like them. I close my eyes. I see death. I open my eyes. A tear falls on my cheek. Anger fills my soul. How did I get here?

Where I Was

6:00 am

Silence. Calm. My eyes open. I prepare for the storm. I stare at the ceiling.

"Coo, coo" the ugly pigeon sings from my balcony.

I pound the window over my bed.

The pigeon, confused, flies off. It returns to plant its fat ass back on my balcony.

"Coo, coo."

Storm. Knives carve through my intestines. I clench my stomach. Fists pound my gut. I gag. An axe swings, shattering my insides. I curse. I groan. I ride it out. An hour passes. I numb the pain. I get up. Not pumped, but groggy and alive. I walk to the bathroom. I ignore the mirror. I shit-shower-shave-brush my teeth. I take a couple of vitamins to build my broken immune system. I don't start work till 4:00 pm. I go for a swim. I work on my research paper for my internship program.

3:30 pm

I look for my keys. My apartment has the appearance of a spacious bachelor's pad. It's my dungeon of isolated hell. I find my keys on the coffee table near an empty vodka bottle. Last night's medicine. I take the elevator downstairs to Jimmy. I ignite Jimmy and head off to my first shift as a specialized services aide. As I drive, I watch summer fade into fall. I unroll my window and inhale the aroma of new beginnings. I tell myself it's a new day. A fresh start. I tell myself I'm not drinking tonight. That I don't need it. I shake my head. False hope. I pull up to the family's house in St. Albert, where I grew up. My phone rings. It's Dad. Dad, Don to others, is a man who exudes confidence. His sun-dyed blond hair, permanent bronzed-skin, dark eyes, and straight pearly white teeth say he's thirty, but really he's an old man in his fifties. He started a plumbing company with a five-thousand dollar loan from his dad. With that money he bought one van and some supplies, and he hired a couple of employees. Twenty years later, he has close to sixty employees, dozens of vans, and has made well over five thousand dollars. He defines success. He takes pride in himself and who he is—something I've always envied.

I pick up my phone.

"Hey, Pops."

"Hey, son, how are you doing?"

"Good, thanks. Just getting to my first shift. How about yourself?"

"Oh, sorry Luke, I didn't know you started work this late … I'll call you after your shift." His voice trembles mid-sentence.

A little concerned, I reply, "No, go ahead Dad. I have a couple minutes. What's up?"

Dad breathes heavily.

"Uncle Gary died this morning at around 6:00 am. You and Dave were the last to see him last night. He died in his sleep."

Uncle Gary was a closet alcoholic. No one knew of his problem with alcohol. Dad clued in, though. He gave Uncle Gary a job in his office and smelled booze on him each morning. Dad expressed his concern to Uncle Gary, but, as all closet drinkers do, Uncle Gary offered countless excuses. It wasn't until recently, when the doctors told us he had cirrhosis of the liver, that we knew how serious and fatal his secret addiction was. The doctors gave him another year to live.

"This really sucks."

"Sure does. I'm sorry you have to take all this news at once." He's referring to last night's dinner, when he told my brother, Dave, and me that he and Mom are officially getting a divorce.

"It's not your fault. I'm sorry for how I reacted last night." I'm referring to my outburst. I called him and Mom liars and said I didn't need to deal with their shit. "And I'm sorry we lost Uncle Gary." He was Dad's second-youngest brother out of eleven siblings and my godfather.

"Me too, son. But he was very sick. He drank at least a two-six of vodka a day. And that's what we know of. It's close to a forty. You can't live like that forever." My uncle wasn't able to get a liver transplant. He was also obese and a smoker. Alcohol killed him first. "What did he say to you guys last night? I wanted to talk about it more at dinner, but it got a little heated."

"Nothing, really. Just a few groans. Eventually he called out my name. His body felt like a stress ball, and he looked yellower from the broken liver. The nurse came in to give him medicine, and it took both of us to lift him up." He's over three hundred pounds. "Dave tried to help him sip coffee, but he had such bad shakes that the coffee spilled on his hospital gown and all he got out was a couple painful groans. It wasn't easy to watch."

"I bet. I'm sorry you had to go through that, son. I'll let you know about the funeral as soon as I get the details."

"Yeah, I should get to work. Don't want to be late for my first shift."

"You're a tough kid. You're the last one I worry about in this situation." Dad doesn't know I drink away my pain every night.

"Thanks, Dad. Talk to you later."

"Bye, son."

I hang up. I crank my tunes. I take a few breaths. I erase my mind of thought. I take one last deep breath. I open the door. I look at my surroundings, so I don't get nailed by a car. I walk to one of my new offices, Connor's house. I meet the family. His parents greet me with welcoming hellos. They seem very happy and together. My supervisor and I hang out with Connor. He seems very intelligent and observant. He's seven. He's a functioning child with autism. He can speak a few word sentences, read and write with verbal prompts, spell like a bee champion, and he is good at math. He also has a special talent for being able to play computer games. He plays games online against young and old gamers and always wins. When the opponent expresses his acknowledgment of talent, Connor's dad replies, saying his kid is autistic and hasn't learned to type.

7:00 pm

Driving home, I think about Uncle Gary. I wasn't expecting him to go that fast. He wasted his life away, but I didn't think alcohol could end it at forty-six. I tense up. My heart pounds. My mind is struck with anger. I punch my steering wheel. *You're next, Luke.* "Fuck off!" I pull into my apartment building's garage. I park Jimmy and head upstairs to the foyer. There's a door that connects to a public underground parking lot, which leads to a variety of stores. The parking lot is my tunnel of hatred. Filled with shame, I only see a shaded, depressing grey. I walk toward the grey back door. I walk through the beer cooler to the hard liquor section. I used to purchase the upscale Smirnoff vodka, but daily transactions have necessitated removing all luxuries. I grab a bottle of Alberta Pure vodka. The regular cashier is an African man in his early thirties who doesn't speak much English. We talk at times. If people are in the store, he senses I don't want to be there. I worry someone will see me. It's empty tonight, considering it's Monday. We speak.

"Any robberies lately?" I ask weird questions.

He smiles. "No, no, not today. Guy yesterday take case of beer out back door. We don't catch him."

"The beer cooler's access to the parkade is a perfect and easy getaway. But don't worry about me; I'll never do it. I'll just be back the next day." We share a laugh. I laugh at myself. He hands me my change.

"Take care." I grab the bag and walk toward the beer cooler. I realize I forgot my backpack to hide it. I wrap the bag around my wrist and palm the bottle.

"You too." He waves.

I go through the beer cooler into the parkade and then into the foyer. I walk into the elevator with two gorgeous girls. They look at me and then at the noticeably hidden bottle in my hand.

"Going to have a good night?" one asks, while the other giggles.

I look down at the bottle. I look up.

"This isn't enough for a good night," I smile.

The elevator stops on floor eight.

"Take care, ladies."

"Bye," they sing in unison.

I unlock the door to my apartment. Vodka surrounds my thoughts. I walk to the black leather couch. I sit and say hi to vodka. I break the ice. I take a swig. The bottle's half empty. I chase it with leftover Sprite that's sitting on the coffee table from last night. My body warms into a comforting bliss. It's not enough. I need more. I grab the bottle. I finish it. My nerves calm. I feel nothing. SportsCenter is on TV. I stare through the highlights. I talk to myself. "So, this is how you did it Uncle Gary? This is how you wasted your life away? Huh? This is what killed you? I can't believe you did this! I fucking hate you!" I throw the plastic bottle against the balcony windows. I'm not satisfied only being thirteen ounces deep. I walk down to the liquor store. There are a couple of people inside. I put my head down and silently grab a bottle. At the till, the cashier and I don't speak. He looks into my eyes. He sees fear and looks down. He knows I'm on the brink. He gives me my change. I turn. I stumble into a display case of wine, knocking one into mid-air. I get a hand on it. I put it back and keep going. I take the stairs. I sit on the couch. I chug half the bottle. No chase. I curse my uncle. I walk onto the balcony. The crisp chill from a sudden wind hits my face. I stare blindly into the sky's deep shade of black. I'm met with anger. Hatred. Weakness. Tears fill my eyes. I apologize to Uncle Gary for cursing him. I talk to him. "Why did you say my name? Why was that all you were able to muster?" I pause. My head drops. "How can you be dead? You're too young. You can't go before Grandpa. You're his best friend, Dad's little bro, my godfather. Fuck!" Anger. Hatred. I grab the bottle. I finish it. I walk to the bathroom. The light is off. I'm sick of my face. I brush my teeth. I rinse. I turn the light on. I look at my face in the mirror. I see nothing. I mumble, "Fuck you." I turn the light off.

9:00 am

Pigeon wakes me up. I'm sprawled on my bed. My blankets are on the ground. I have no shirt on. My pants are on. I feel the silence. I prepare for the storm. Knives carve. Axes swing. Fists punch. I clench my stomach. I gag. I cough. I groan. Misery.

08/30/07, Uncle Gary's Funeral

I don't feel comfortable about already having to miss a day of work to go to a funeral. Mostly, I don't want to face Uncle Gary's death. When Dad told me the time of the funeral, I said I had to work. He said to get the day off. I called my supervisor and said I had a funeral, but I can skip it for work. She said to go to the funeral. I decide to go to the funeral.

10:00 am

I wake up. Silence. Storm Knives. Stomach Gag. Clench. I grimace. I ride it out. Half an hour passes. I get up. Today, I get to listen to someone who didn't know Uncle Gary preach God and death. I shit-shower-shave and put on my suit. I leave for the funeral.

4:00 pm

The funeral service was decent. The youngest sibling, Uncle Todd, shared funny stories. I liked it. As Gary's godson, I was asked to read a prayer. I thought the prayer sucked. I read it. I sobbed during "Let it be" by the Beatles. Dave gave me a look of concern. I told him I was okay. I smiled. I went back to my tunnel of thought with silent tears. I know I'm following Uncle Gary's footsteps. I know what will kill me. Only I know. Now Uncle Gary does, too. I cry, knowing I'll die. Dave thinks the tears are of mourning. They're tears of horror. Fear. Sickness. Desperation. Anger. Powerlessness. Hopelessness. Sadness. Fear.

5:00 pm

We're on our way to Sorrentino's in St. Albert for dinner. I'm driving alone. I want to be alone. I'm furious. I'm sick. I'm angry. So fucking angry. I crank my tunes. I drive. I ignore scenery. I park Jimmy. Fifteen of us sit down at a large table. I sit beside Dad, with Mom across from me. Beside Mom is Grandpa Dick. I love that man. The waitress comes to our table. I'm staring numbly at my napkin.

"Hi, guys. I'm Grace. I'll be serving you tonight."

That voice sounds familiar. I look up. That smile. Those eyes. It's her. I reflect on the first time we met. It was at a "Dawn till Dusk" charity golf tournament a couple of months ago. I was golfing and she was volunteering as a beer cart girl for Sorrentino's. After ten hours of golfing and drinking I was done golfing for the day. I hung out with the Sorrentino girls. We sat on our carts. We drank and chatted. Once Grace and I made eye contact, I was struck with her bright blue eyes and beautiful smile. I then found out she had a boyfriend. I'm not up for talking and when we met I was hammered. I go back to my napkin. I find myself looking up again. Our eyes meet. The hair on the back of my neck gets an erection.

"I'll have a pint of Kokanee please." I say with a smile.

"Sure thing." Grace smiles back.

After food and a couple of pints, I say my goodbyes. I want to say bye to Grace. I don't. Gutless. I want to be alone. I want to drink in peace. Vodka, a couch, and a wall will accomplish that.

5:00 am

I wake up. Silence is my alarm. Storm. Axe. Intestines. Bathroom. Puke. Stomach Clench. Curse. I stumble to bed. I lie down. I stare at the ceiling. Last night was bad. I burned my knuckle. I was drunk while cooking chicken. Oil splashed on my knuckle and legs. I was in my boxers. I attended to my legs. I didn't feel the oil on my knuckle. Alcohol numbs pain. Now it's blistered and going to put me behind in boxing. I had cooked chicken and shrimp. I choked on a piece of chicken. I couldn't cough. I tried to flush it down with my glass of milk. I couldn't swallow it. Milk spilled onto my chin and shirt. My eyes watered. I wasn't crying. I had no thoughts. I took my right hand, made a fist, and pumped my stomach. I stuck my index finger down my throat. Time passed. I felt lightheaded. My vision blurred. I used all my force. I dislodged it. It landed on my plate. I gasped for air. I sat motionless, staring at the wall. I wiped away my tears. I had no thoughts. I wiped the milk off my mouth. I threw away the food. I changed my shirt. I sat on the couch. I grabbed the bottle. I drank. I later stumbled into the wall and fell on my face. I have a cut with dried blood on my forehead. I puked and then bought more booze. I had wasted it on puking. I cursed my uncle. I woke up on my hallway floor fully clothed. Vodka kicked my ass. Again. Defeated. Again. This relationship is getting out of control. I'm miserable.

09/29/07, Random Night

12: 07 am

Tonight I bought a bottle of wine, hoping to soften the hangovers. I thought I would fall asleep. I drank it and went to bed at 10:30 pm. I couldn't sleep. At midnight, I ran downstairs to the liquor store. The back door to the beer cooler was locked. I rushed to the front of the store. The African man was outside, locking the door. I ran up to him and asked if I could quickly buy a bottle. He said the register was closed. He looked at me, saw desperation, looked inside, and told me to grab a bottle and pay him tomorrow. I did and thanked him. I walked back home, relieved I had gotten my booze. Now I sit and reflect. I'm met with fear. I fear sleep without alcohol. It's controlling me. I'm powerless. The bottle has become my mistress. I'm an expected customer. I'm a regular. I grab the bottle. I chug. *What's it going to take, Luke?* "Fuck if I know. I don't think anything can make me stop drinking. Maybe rehab, but I can't blow my cover. It's embarrassing. I can fix it on my own." *You're losing it, Luke. Go see a shrink.* "What can a shrink do? I know I have a problem. I've identified it. I'll fix it." *Even shrinks need shrinks, Luke. You can't do this on your own. It doesn't work that way.* "I can fix this on my own. It's not permanent." *Then at least see a shrink as research for your career.* "It's a thought. Maybe talking to someone in confidentiality will help." *You might like it.* "I wouldn't say that much." I finish the bottle. I go to bed. I pass out.

10/06/07, Session One: Doubt

9:00 am

I park Jimmy a block from the building. Walking toward it, I survey its appearance. Bricked and aged, it gives off the essence of business. I approach the building. The sense of business shifts to illness. I walk inside. The air smells of rehabilitation for the mentally ill. I take the elevator to floor seven and find the office labelled "46" at the end of the hall. I walk up to the reception desk. The receptionist is in her early thirties. She looks timid but unsatisfied with her placement. I tell her my name. She looks up without a smile. She tells me to take a seat. I nod. I take a seat in the waiting room. I'm a patient with mental illness—this doesn't help the ego. I pick up a *Times* magazine. I give the illusion I'm reading. I go over in my head the process that's about to happen. I'll get the confidentiality speech. Everything I say he has to keep to himself, unless he has reason to believe I'll cause harm to myself or others. He'll then ask me why I seek his help. He'll ask me a few questions regarding what he feels my issue might be. Once we classify me, we will move on to the intervention process. The intervention process will consist of working on a cognitive level to help me through such issues. There are many therapeutic routes to take. Every psychologist is different.

Dr. Handman walks into the waiting room. I met him as a child. He referred me to a child psychologist. He sees me in his peripherals, glances over, gives an expression of recognition, and greets me with a welcoming hello. He's a fit, well-dressed man in his mid-fifties. Grey hairs are sprouting on the side of his scalp. His smile is shaped by happiness and confidence. The light in his dark brown eyes gazes respect. Important qualities. However, I ignore first impressions. I've learned that from myself.

"Hey, how's it going?" I stand up to shake his hand.

"I'm good, thanks. How are you, Luke?"

"I wouldn't be here if I was pumped," I say, jokingly.

He smiles.

"Why don't we go to my office?"

"Sounds good."

I follow him to his office. On the way, I examine the area. A few other psychologists' offices make a path to his office. Pictures of panoramic mountains and forests brighten the trail. His office is in the back corner. As I step into his office, I look to the right. A large window paints the view of Edmonton's downtown district. Below the window is a desk filled with papers, pens, and literature. Above and to the right are certificates and diplomas of credentials. Against the wall to the right of his desk is a bookcase devoted to books on disorders and dysfunctions. To the left of his desk is a green La-Z-Boy used for hypnosis. I walk toward his desk, check his view, walk back to where two leather seats are, and sit in what I suppose is the shrinkee's chair.

"It's good to see you, Luke. I'm happy you've chosen to come see me. I remember you from when you were a little kid. I've always liked you, but you didn't seem to like me so much back then," he says jokingly.

"Yeah, sorry about that." I don't remember. I've repressed those days. "Nice office."

"Thanks. So I will start by saying that everything you say is confidential …"A minute later, "I'm going to ask you a couple of questions. At the end of the session, you let me know if you want to keep having appointments, or I can refer you to someone else."

"Sounds good."

"When you called in, you told the receptionist that you may be depressed."

"Yeah, and if it were more serious I wouldn't be telling your receptionist, who hasn't fed me the confidentiality speech."

He pauses.

"How's your sleep?"

"Insomniac since childhood."

"How's your appetite?"

"I never eat in the morning. My stomach doesn't allow it. My first meal ranges between noon and seven."

"How's your concentration?"

"No worse than the average person claiming to have ADD."

He smiles. He gets it. He goes back to business.

"How's your sex drive?"

"A few short-term relationships. Nothing serious. I can get it up, if that's what you're asking," I smile.

He laughs. He goes back to business.

"Well, Luke. There's a good chance you have clinical depression. If you would like I can refer you to a doctor for anti-depressants."

"No, not for me. I came to see you because I want to work on my mind, not to repress shit with drugs." I got alcohol for that.

"Sure, that is what we will do. Would you like to try hypnosis for your sleep?"

"Yeah, I'll give it a shot."

"Okay, Luke, so what do you think? Do you want to stick around? We will have a few sessions of therapy and hypnosis to build you back up."

"Sounds all right." I get up. We set a time. We shake hands.

"See you later," he says as I walk out.

Walking to Jimmy, I consider my decision to seek help. I feel I'm doing the right thing. I'm conflicted. I feel I'm just wasting my parents' money. I don't see myself telling this guy the truth. *You're slowly dying.* "I'm doing what you told me to do." *You aren't going to tell him about your drinking.* "I don't know the guy." *You better tell him, Luke. Alcoholism is going to kill you.* "I'm not an alcoholic. I can fix this. I'm smart. I'm young." *This is out of your control.* "Fuck that nonsense. I'm in full control of my life." *So was your uncle.* "Go to hell." I tell the back of my mind to beat it. I drive to work.

7:25 pm

I grab my black Adidas gym bag from my trunk. I grab my blue Ringside boxing gloves.

I joined boxing after I got home from Montreal and got a place in Edmonton. I went to Montreal for a year of university after high school. In Montreal, I lived in the "ghetto" area drenched with old rusted buildings, signs breaking at the seams, and ratty people exhausted by broken dreams muttering regrets. I lived alone in a sound-echoing one-bedroom apartment. My bathroom was the colour of an aged sky, rusted blue. My friends residing in McGill dorms lived thirty minutes by bus from my apartment. I attended Concordia University and walked a half hour to the lecture halls in the icy chill from Montreal's damp winters. It would take me another half hour to defrost. At night, I frequented the run-down liquor store regularly, drinking away isolation. Consumed with boredom, I read a lot. My favourite book was *The Power of One,* by Bryce Courtenay. It's about this kid who used boxing as an outlet during an oppressive childhood. I liked the book. When I moved back to Edmonton, I joined Panther Gym to box. The trainers are smart fighters. I learn a lot from them. They say I have talent. My power and speed are my strengths, and my footwork from past athletics is a plus. Panther's in a basement below a vet's clinic. Not the war heroes. The sick pets. Boxing is a challenge. An individual, only-the-strong-survive Darwin mentality. Panther has a good atmosphere. A lack of central air-conditioning fills the air with testosterone and our bodies with sweat. Old duct-taped punching bags personify the sport as it is: old school. Kids from suburban living, broken homes, and bad environments receive education about sport and living from well-trained fighters who have lived their past and have come out of it strong. We're all friends, and we fight. Like a family. It gets intense, but, at the end of the day, it's all to help each other's technique to fight the competition. I want to get serious and join the amateur team. I want to get into scheduled fights. I know I can't be competitive until I cut down on my drinking. For now I train with the open class, or by myself, and spar when asked. I want to spar today. It releases anger.

"I'm so fast that last night I turned the light switch off in my bedroom and I was in bed before the room was dark," I mumble to myself, as I walk across the street. Those are the words of my favourite boxer, Muhammad "The Greatest" Ali, three-time heavyweight champion of the world. He's the smoothest fighter I have ever seen and a cultural icon. I like boxing.

10/20/07, Session Two: Repressed Pain

7:20 am

I wake up. Calm storm. Stomach clench. Gag. Anger. Curse. Axe. Clench. Anger—so much fucking anger! I hate it. I hate this. I'm motionless. I have to see a stranger, I mean shrink, I mean psychiatrist, I mean psychologist. Same shit. I have to tell him my repressed memories. I have to relive my past. I have to trust him. I can hate him. He has to tell me what to do. He has to tell me the truth. He has to give it to me straight. I can say whatever I want. I'm paying him. I can be whoever I want. Who would want to be a shrink?

7:50 am

I walk up the stairs to the building. I'm a patient, I mean client. *You want to be a shrink, but you can't even take care of yourself.* "I'm fine. This is research, remember?" *Shut up, Luke. You know that was bullshit.* I get off the elevator and walk toward the office. I take a seat in the waiting room. I'm a couple of minutes early. I pick up a *Times* magazine. I read a section about global warming. Apparently methane gas from cow's farts is a big contributor. The more meat we eat, the more cows we need, the more cows there are to fart, which heats the air with their methane stench. Supply and demand. Red meat is delicious. When I'm done reading the article, I look at the clock. It's 8:06 am. If someone is going to be late it should be me, not him. There he is. It's about time.

"Hey, Luke. I'm sorry I'm a little behind."

"I could be sleeping." I ignore his eyes. I walk past him toward his office. I take a seat in the same chair as last time.

Dr. Handman takes a seat across from me.

"So, you say you are feeling depressed these days. Do you have any idea of why this is happening?"

He has a drinking problem.

"Ever since I was young, I've struggled with adversity, alongside self-loathing. You know me from when I was a kid, so you know I was given the raw end of the deal."

"Yes, absolutely. You were in rough shape, but you always seemed to be optimistic."

"Or so I let on. Every day was different. I don't really know how I was feeling then. I would be optimistic, and then things would take a turn for the worse. I couldn't get out of bed for a month, and sometimes I'd end up in the hospital."

"Yeah, that must have been tough. Are you still facing issues from your childhood today?"

"Well, I can't say I'm over it. I've done well at repressing my issues." With vodka. Or wine. I like rye, too. Beer, of course, but that's a special occasion. It's too weak with too many calories to drink daily. I stick with scentless vodka.

"Well, how about we go back into your childhood and work through the memories. When is your earliest memory of the whole thing?"

"Umm." Tough question. "Tough question. I don't remember this, but my parents have told me that I was nine months old around the time I started developing eczema. It wasn't too much to worry about in the beginning, just a few rashes, cuts, and dry skin patches. But, as time passed, it got worse. From two to twelve, it started adding up all over my body to the point of causing immobility. I remember the intense physical pain I felt on a daily basis. I remember the feeling of complete anger and being furious with God and his sick, twisted mind. I remember looking into Mom's eyes and seeing the reflection of a broken heart. A shattered soul. She blamed herself and wanted my pain, so I wouldn't have to suffer. I remember watching Dad and my brother, Dave, back me up each day, but I saw the pain in their eyes, too. My family is special. They wanted my pain." I pause. I lean back in my chair. I cross my left leg over my right, faking sophistication in my Under Armour sweats and Panther Gym hoodie. I hide my pain. "When it comes down to one's own physical pain and the emotional struggle of a mother, there isn't a comparison. I wasn't worried about Dad and Dave. They're strong guys. But Mom … Mom has a soft heart, a beautiful soul. She was there every minute of my pain. I was comforted knowing I had the skin condition and not her, because I knew I was in control of dealing with the physical aspect. But to see the pain in her eyes ..." I stop. I hate this. I feel weak. I repress my thoughts. I unravel my sweats to scratch my leg. I look at the hallmark white scars covering my skin, permanent reminders of the past. I look up. I look into Handman's eyes. "I think that's good enough for today, Dr. Handman. Let's try that hypnosis stuff. I can use a nap before work."

He stares into my eyes.

I put on a mask.

He digs for my thoughts.

"Are you sure, Luke? Those were some very interesting comments you just made. It'll help to keep talking about it. I know there is a lot of pain there. If you are sure, we will move on to the hypnosis."

"Sounds good, doc. Where do I sit? In that puke green La-Z-boy over there?" I say jokingly, pointing to the ugly chair. I don't think I like this shrink idea.

8:00 pm

I'm in my apartment sitting on the couch, bottle in hand. I've been thinking of a way to heal myself from drinking alone. I've photocopied my medical file from my physician. I have a box of journals, writings, and notes from my childhood. I have to figure out what's wrong with me. I haven't gotten far. The bottle in hand speaks for itself. I remember when Handman asked me about sex during that first session. My answer reminds me of my meaningless past relationships. Maybe I need to find my first love, and I can get over this burden. I reflect on my past.

I've never had a real relationship. The last girl I dated was a bed buddy turned girlfriend. That wasn't going to last. When she ended it, because she caught on that I'm a prick, I told her she was the drunkest girl in St. Albert and just another slut.

I fell for one girl; her name was Megan. She was out of my league, a perfect ten: beauty and mind. We met at a bar through a buddy. My buddy had a big crush on her. He gave us the speech on how hot she was before she got there. We talked. I charmed her. I got her number. Her personality was more attractive than her natural beauty. She was one of a rare breed. We shared tons of laughs and talked about everything there is to talk about. We talked about life. We never fought. But we also never dated. She had an ex from Lethbridge who she wasn't over. He was five years older than me, four years older than her. She had a hard time with the age thing. She had only dated older guys. We spent time together for eight months. We both went to the University of Alberta, and we had a class together. We hung out regularly at my condo downtown. We both knew she wasn't over her past and agreed we wouldn't date till she let go of her baggage. I knew I was a distraction from her breakup. I knew it couldn't work, but I couldn't resist her sex appeal and personality. With time, and no progress, the drama began. She would say she was going to a lake for the weekend, but she would end up in Lethbridge seeing her ex. One night, her ex got hold of her phone. He called me. We talked. Nice guy. He asked if I was kissing his girl. I said yes, I was kissing his ex. He said "Cool, have a good one." I said the same. Twenty minutes later, Megan called me from a payphone. She called to tell me she had lost her phone. I said, "Don't worry; I know who found it." I told her she was a waste of my time and hung up. The next morning, I got a call that Jeremy, a friend of our family, had died. He was twenty-four and a great lacrosse and hockey player, friend, husband, son, and brother. He had many goals and ambitions. He was going to go pro for lacrosse, but melanoma cancer took his life. It's bullshit. No logic behind it. Good people should never die young. His soul lives on. Megan called me an hour later and tried to reason with me. I said I didn't care to deal with her garbage. But I told her to come over. I needed a friend. We hung out that day. You can say I was dumb, but I knew she would always be a friend. After it ended for good, we didn't speak for a couple of years. Now we keep in touch as friends. The way it was meant to be.

Out of my one-night stands I could recognize one girl. Last summer, when I was living in downtown Edmonton, I occasionally went to this neighbourhood pub called Docks. My parents owned the condo, so I had three friends living with me at various intervals to help me with the costs. In between, and at the end, I had the place to myself. When I did have a roommate, I would tell him or her that I was going for midnight walks. The walk was ten steps to my seat at the bar, to watch sport highlights or play VLTs. One of the waitresses was this petite brunette. I'll call her Stacy. I knew she wasn't beer-goggle hot, because I would initially arrive at the pub sober. When Stacy worked, we would make small talk. I had considered taking her back to my place, but I knew it had the potential to blow my cover. It would be rude not to introduce her to my roommate. How would I explain what she did? So I shrugged it off. But as time went on, the flirting hit a climax—pun intended. I was living alone, because my parents had sold the place, and I was about to move out. This funny gay couple I would sometimes drink with told me the girl had had a crush on me for months. I asked them if I should go for it. The obviously gay one (must wear the panties) said, "Oh my God—you totally should. I bet she would totally be a great lay." He was very enthusiastic. I looked at him and let out a laugh I had attempted to hold back. I said, "Really? You think about having sex with girls?" I looked at his straight-looking partner (must wear the boxers) and said, "Watch out for this one. He might be swinging for both teams." He laughed, "Are you kidding? Look at him. Gay as a gay guy can get." We all burst into laughter. That night we got drunk with Stacy. She was friends with them. I brought her to my place. We slept together. The next day I was hung over and rude. She left in anger. It was a good thing I moved out a week later. It would have made drinking at that pub awkward. That's my sex life: meaningless.

No shit, it's meaningless. I take a swig. If I find true love, maybe I won't need to drink alone. Something has to change. *You called a girl a slut? Did you read that, dipshit? You're a joke.* "I've done nothing compared to lots of guys and even girls I know." *Comparing yourself to the slutty people won't do you any good. Why don't you compare yourself to the guys in a committed healthy relationship?* "I would, but I haven't found a girl worth dating." *Because you sleep with them the first night. You need to find a lady and go on a date. You're smart, Luke, come on.* "Not in relationships." *You need to quit drinking before you get in a relationship.* "No. Other way around. Love will fix me."

9:00 am

The receptionist tells me Dr. Handman is ready for me in his office.

"Thank you." I get up from my seat. I walk toward his office. I stop for a tea. I walk into his office.

"Hey, what's up, Dr. Handman?" I dip the tea bag. I'm feeling good today. I didn't drink much last night. I was really tired. I only had a mickey.

"Hey, Luke, you're looking happier today," he says in a satisfied tone.

"Yeah, I'm doing great, thanks. Feel like I can run a marathon." I take a seat.

"Speaking of which, how about we talk about sports today? I remember you being a dedicated basketball player when you were younger. Want to share some sports stories?"

"You're singing my tune, my friend. What do you want to hear?"

"Well, how about we start with your love for the game, and you can work in your eczema at free will."

"All right, let's do that." I rub my hands on my sweats. I take a deep breath and mould myself into the black leather. "Well, I didn't initially want to be a basketball player. I was supposed to be a hockey player. Family background, big hockey neighbourhood, friends were all hockey players. I wanted to be a goalie, like my old man, but, with the equipment, my skin couldn't breathe, making it unbearable. And my asthma would react badly to the sport. So, my next choice was football. I tried that out for a bit. I was on a team with my bro, my best buddy Matt, and my cousin. We practiced two months in the summer prior to our first game. I was a safety. Wicked position. I got to read the offense and make the tackle. As in hockey, I reacted to the equipment, and being allergic to grass was a drawback, to say the least. But I muscled through it, because, at that point in my life, I had two passions: sports and candy. One of my many random doctors had advised me sugar made my skin worse, so I was on a sugar-free diet. I wasn't going to let sports be taken away. And I didn't, but some doctor did. He was my breathing doctor, who helped me relax. Well, that day, he set me off, contradicting his profession. He told my mom that, for the benefit of everyone, it would be best I didn't play football. Mom knew this. She also knew how much football meant to me. But she saw how bad my skin was getting, and she agreed. I cursed them then, though I thank them now. But this was a week before my first game, Handman. That really pissed me off."

"Dr. Handman," he corrects me.

"Oh, sorry. Anyhow, after football, I tried many sports. Karate failed, because my skin would crack mid-kick, leaving blood on the mat. It got embarrassing. I didn't like soccer, and the grass set off my asthma and skin. I always enjoyed playing hoops, though. When I was about six, I started shooting the ball around. At eight, I decided to join a camp at the University of Alberta coached by the Golden Bears. The starting age was nine, but we begged, and they let me play. I was one of the smallest on the court, but I battled hard. I had a knack for the game. I remember that first camp specifically, because it was there I was told I had talent. At the end of the camp, they held a ceremony to hand out awards to the MVPs and contest winners and such. A few hundred people—family, friends, and the ball players—filled the bleachers. I wasn't expecting a thing. I was just happy to be sitting beside my big brother and a couple of buddies I had met in camp. I shouldn't have belonged, but I did, because I had proved myself on the court." I stop talking to take a sip of tea. Memories flood my mind. My heart beats a soft rhythm. I feel pride. "As the night was winding down, my coach for that camp, Omar, got up in front of the microphone. And he said, I impersonate, 'We have a special award to give out tonight, folks. This will be a one-time thing. The entire coaching staff got together and decided one little guy deserves to be recognized for his strength. We call this award the Courage in the Face of Adversity Award. It goes out to a special little man, who, although he was the smallest on the court, never backed down and always fought hard for the ball and was a big team player.'" I stop for a breather. This is the most memorable moment of my childhood. "And I just remember thinking, 'Wow, this guy must have made a big impact. Good for him.' And then, Omar continues, 'Luke Tougas, could you make your way to the court, please?' I look at my brother. His face is lit up with pride. I look across the aisle toward my parents. Mom is crying like a baby, and Dad has a smile from ear to ear; he's shocked as hell. He knew I was good, but this recognition was remarkable. I stood up. The players were hollering my name, patting me on the back, giving me high-fives. All of a sudden, everyone stands up and gives me a standing ovation, a first and last, that night. I was on top of the world, man." I'm in that moment. I smile. "I had been through so much pain at that point. To be honoured for courage in the face of adversity couldn't have been a better fit. That day changed my outlook on life. Just goes to show the impact of sport." I look Dr. Handman in the eyes. I give him a head nod with a smirk.

He smiles back. A couple guys talking sports. Handman's a sports fan. A Habs fan for hockey and a general football fan. Oilers are a better choice, but still good, and being a football fan puts him above the bar. I'm starting to like this guy. I feel I can talk to him.

"But that's about it, doc." My smirk quickly fades into depression. Anxiety, resentment, and distress are in sight. "That's in the past. All I'm left with are some trophies and scars. Somehow, I feel my life was better as a dried blood, cutup body with something to fight through. Now, I'm just older and broken."

"You're in school to be a psychologist, right?"

"Yeah."

"You're pursuing your goal. You should be proud."

"One would think. I've never felt that word, pride. Maybe when I was playing ball, but not today. I know on paper I'm ambitious and doing what is needed to become a future psychologist, but inside ... well, inside it's a dark hole waiting for disaster. I don't know how to describe it. I would tell you if I knew." *You know.* "Anyhow, I enjoyed this session. It was nice to look back at that U of A camp. Great memory."

Handman softly smiles with pity.

I get up. "Take care, Dr. Handman."

Handman gets up. We shake hands. He nods. "You, too, Luke."

Time for work.

7:00 pm

I ignite Jimmy. I drive home. I have one thought. I park Jimmy. I walk down my tunnel. My mind told me not to all day. I agreed. I follow my footsteps. I told myself I wouldn't take this walk. I continue down my tunnel. I pick up the mistress. I greet the African man. We chat. I said it a dozen times—I'm not taking this walk. I pay. We say goodbye. I walk the stairs to floor eight to be alone with the mistress. I told myself all day I wouldn't do it. I break the seal. I obsessed all day about not doing it. I chug.

12:20 am

I wake up. My head bobs. I'm sitting straight up in my accustomed drinking seat. I blink a few times to remove the blur. Slowly, the landscape comes into focus, illuminating the balcony windows. I gaze at the moon's glow beaming off the small house shackled between a twenty-nine-storey apartment and a ten-storey business building, captive in its home. I realize it's night. I dozed off. I look at the bottle. It's half empty. I chug. I'm reminded of my uncle. Alcohol's the trigger. The bottle has been replaced with his soul. I throw the bottle against the wall, leaving a black shaded scar. I stare at the wall. I stand and walk toward the balcony. I lean my arm against the balcony window, head bend in defeat. I reflect.

I'm going to die young. I'm accepting it. I treat my body like a garbage disposal. I haven't been the greatest person. I'm a shitty brother. I'm a fraud, not a son. My parents pay for my education. I drink away my future in secrecy. I smile in appreciation when people call me Dr. Luke, making reference to my future goal. I laugh in my head, knowing I'm a pathetic failure. I don't give a shit. I am a failure. On paper, I had helped dozens of kids as a youth intervention worker for a couple years, working with kids in group homes, foster homes, and broken homes. At the same time, I feel that leaving those kids behind only added to their problems. They had someone to look up to. For many, it was the first time in their lives. And then I got up and left. This would be a regular occurrence for them. I left them, because I couldn't handle the politics anymore. I enjoyed the work, and I thought the kids were great, but there was too much crap to deal with outside of work. Dealing with foster and group home parents can be a pain, depending if they are in it to pay the bills or if they are truly good people. I met one truly good foster mom.

A buddy of mine got hit by a train. His voices, caused by schizophrenia, told him to do so. The authorities didn't identify the cause of death. They didn't know if it was an accident or suicide. It was neither. It was his voices. He wasn't suicidal. He was found shortly after he escaped his psych ward. He wasn't taking his meds. His voices weren't an accident. I had asked to see him in the psych ward. His voices were telling him to kill the staff. They wouldn't let me see him. I knew he wouldn't kill me. I knew he wouldn't attack me. I was his brother when in need. He had many dreams. He was happy. We worked together once a week for six months. The group home staff was happy Tiger finally had someone he felt he could trust. Toward the end of his life, he got rid of his bad influences. He started to exercise and run to school. He wanted to join the army when he turned eighteen. The army would have been blessed to have Tiger.

I open the sliding door and walk onto the balcony. I stare down the sky. I wipe away weakness. I miss you, Tiger. I look down the eight storeys at the life-ending cement. At the age of twenty-one, I failed at my profession. I close my eyes. I see Tiger. I open my eyes. A tear falls on my cheek. I stumble inside. I stumble to the bathroom. I brush my teeth in darkness. My mind shifts to thoughts of Uncle Gary. I rinse. I punch the door. I shake. I crumble to the floor. I sit against the bathtub. I become stone. Weakness. Sadness. *I miss you, Uncle Gary.* I mute my inner thoughts. A bitter taste of reality sets in. Anger creeps into thought. Alcohol killed you. You chose alcohol. You killed you. My soul darkens. Alcohol's killing me. I choose alcohol. I'm killing myself. My life is my alcohol. Half empty. I get up. I stumble to my king-sized bed. Built for a perfect sleep. I pass out.

11/17/07, Windex Window Cleaner Eyes

It's my buddy's birthday at Oil Slick. I don't care to go out to drink. I'd rather drink alone. I'm safe in my secret. However, close buddies' birthdays are an exception. Since all my friends live in St. Albert or across the city, I'm going to meet them there. I like this. I can chug half a bottle alone before the bar.

9:00 pm

I walk downstairs to the parkade. I see the colours: the yellow dividers, the red, black, blue, green, and white cars. The freshly polished black pavement. It's the weekend. Guilt doesn't consume my thoughts. The shade of grey is replaced with colour. I'm approved by society's rules of function to drink on weekends—when I go out. I walk with my head up to the cooler door. I grab a bottle of Alberta Pure. I look at others: some dressed for a night out, some I see regularly ready to drink away another night of pain. I smile at others. I purchase the bottle of vodka. I tell the African man to have a great night. I decide to walk outside to the front of my apartment building, exposing myself for the world to see. I take the elevator and make small talk. "Going to have a good night?" they ask. "Sure am," is my reply. No hiding for me. I get to my apartment and hop in the shower. As I count the countries on my globe shower curtain, I chug half the bottle. I finish getting ready and stash the other half for when I get home. I call a cab. I get in. I talk to the cab driver. I make small talk about his life. I ask how he got here from India. He tells me of a journey. He tells me about his family. Diversity fascinates me. We get to the bar. I pay the cab driver. I tell him I wish the best for him and his family in Canada. He tells me I'm a good kid. I laugh. That line always makes me laugh. First impressions. I get out of the cab. I say goodbye. The line is jam-packed. The bar is empty. Outside, in the nut-shrinking cold, it's a zoo. Marketing bullshit. I hate bars. I sneak to the front. I hand the bouncer a twenty. I waste my money. I get in. I get the homoerotic pat-down. I walk into the bar. I spot my buddies.

"Tougas! Let's get a shot!" Funk yells across the bar, waving me over.

I say hey to a few buddies and head toward Funk.

"Let's do it up, birthday boy. Two Jager bombs and two Kokanees, please," I ask the sexy bartender.

She hands us our drinks. I pay her. She hands me six loonies, overtly looking for a tip. I hate being given excess change. I reach into my pocket and toss in a quarter. I tip her. We shoot the shots. The Jager warms my insides. I'm comforted. We "cheers!" and sip our beers.

"So, any hot ladies tonight?"

"A few." Funk checks out the surroundings. "There are a few lookers in that group of girls," he says, veering toward a circle of five girls in their early twenties. One girl with natural curly blonde hair turns her head. She catches my eye. My heart pounds. Holy shit, it's her. I wonder if she still has a boyfriend.

"Man, check out that taller blonde over there. I've seen her around a few times. I've had a little crush on her since this golf tournament."

"Then go talk to her, you pansy," Funk eggs me on.

"Hey, pal, don't you worry about me," I say confidently. Thanks, hooch.

"What are you waiting for, hot shot?"

"Ease up bud—in due time. In the meantime, let's get you shitfaced so you forget you were born this day twenty-two years ago." I turn toward the boys. "Hey guys, get over here—shots!" A dozen of us take over the corner bar. We toss away five bucks a shot. We drink and laugh. We catch up. When asked where I've been I repeat the extended truth: focusing on school. An hour passes. I feel loose. I tell Funk we should do a round. We circle about. I see her. The back of my mind works with me. *All right, Luke, go talk to her.*

You've spoken before; it's not like she's a stranger. Say hi and find out if she has a boyfriend. What is Funk doing?

"Hey. Grace, is it?" Funk asks, leaning in for a handshake.

Did I tell him her name?

"Hey, how's it going?" Grace says in a sweet voice.

"This is my buddy, Luke." He tilts his head toward me.

"Hey." That's it? *Rough.*

"Hey," Grace softly replies. We smile in silence. I look into her blue angelic eyes. I can't find words. Grace breaks the ice.

"I saw you at Sorrentino's a while ago and was hoping you were going to talk to me."

"Yeah, I'm sorry about that. I can't say it was the best of days. My mind was out of sorts." Out of sorts? *Oh, man!*

"Oh, I'm sorry to hear that. You did seem a little shy."

"Ha ha, yeah, I am at times. So how's your night going, Grace? Are you and your girlfriends partying tonight?"

"We sure are. They're all over the place. I think some of the girls went to Stonehouse, but a couple of us are thinking of just sticking around here."

"Yeah, you should stick around here. I hear this is the place to be, you know, since we're both here." Off night. *No kidding.*

Grace giggles at my cheesy line. She stares into my eyes.

"Yeah, I think we might."

All right, I've had enough. Find out.

"So, where's your boyfriend tonight?"

"We broke up."

"Oh, that's too bad." My mind dances. I hold in a smile.

"Yeah, he kissed that girl right over there." She turns and points to a blonde girl.

"Really? Only a fool would cheat on you."

Grace smiles. "You're sweet. But no, he kissed her shortly after I broke up with him."

"Oh, I see." I don't get it. "Well, we don't have to talk about that. All that matters is that you look happy and beautiful tonight."

"Aw, thanks, Luke." She touches my arm softly. "I heard you were a good guy."

"It's a mask. Ha ha, I'm only kidding." *If only she* thought you were with me on this one?" *So, you can learn*

I notice someone wobbling in my peripheral vision. I l Funk patiently watches us talk. He steps toward us. He notices Grace has a camera on her arm. He pokes her on the shoulder, like the drunken birthday boy he should be.

"Let me take a picture of youze two," he manages to slur out.

Grace and I look into each other's eyes. We smile and shrug our shoulders. Funk fumbles with the camera. He snags it and takes a picture.

"Well, we should get back to our buddies." I want to leave on a good note. "I'm sorry to hear about you and your boyfriend. Don't worry, though. Everything will work out in the end. How about I get your number and we can hang out sometime?"

"I'd like that." She grabs my phone and adds her number. She hands it back to me. Our eyes meet.

"Take care, Grace."

"See ya, Luke."

Funk and I walk back to the group. We drink.

2:20 am

I get home. I grab the cause of my pain. I grab the solution to my pain. I chug. On any given day, millions of people suffer with addictions. It eases the pain of broken lives. It's a temporary solution that creates permanent problems. It's a vicious cycle of hell and pain. I've read dozens of case studies and books on alcoholism. Its messed up how a store-bought substance can ruin lives. People can develop mental insanity from excessive alcohol use and end up in mental institutions. People can have alcohol-induced seizures from excessive use. People can die from a broken liver. Those are a few of many consequences of long-term use. The immediate effects are the everyday excuses. Alcohol is an excuse when a couple fights in public, when couples cheat on each other, when marriages are torn, when children are abused, when people commit murder, when lives are lost, ruined, or wasted away—alcohol is the excuse. When someone drives drunk and kills someone, alcohol is the excuse. When a crime is committed and intoxication is a factor, alcohol is an excuse to lessen a sentence in court. Alcohol is a gateway from trying. It's an easy way out. Alcohol is a depressant to treat depression. Alcohol is a legal drug. Alcohol is very accessible and addictive. I don't have an addiction. I'm fixing it before it becomes one. I'm aware. I'm oblivious. I'm torn. I'm angry. I'm scared. I'm sad. I'm hopeless. I'm angry—so fucking angry. I hate the world. The world is fucked. The solution is clear: inhale, inject, swallow, sniff. In my case: chug.

Saturday night is my favourite solitary drunk night. No work tomorrow. NFL Sunday. My religion. My hangover healer. I go see the African man. I grab a two-six of Alberta Pure and a can of Sprite for chase. A few people called me to go out. I stick to my updated excuse. I'm working on my internship research paper for my Internship Psychology program at school. I take a couple of swigs. I decide to go on *Facebook*. I log in and notice I've been tagged in a picture. I click on the notification. It's a picture of me and Grace at Oil Slick. I have one arm around her, the other holding a Kokanee; our faces are touching, and Grace is twirling her hair. I like it. Why did Jordanne tag me in this picture? I'll text Grace to see what's up. "Hey, Grace, it's Luke. Just got tagged in that picture of us. Too cool to tag me yourself. Ha ha, jk."

You have to start talking to girls when you're sober.

Twenty minutes and a couple of swigs later, *beep.* "Ha ha, yeah, apparently I can't add you. I think you're the one that's too cool, ha ha."

Say something legit and get out. "Can't argue with that. I'll add you. Have a great night, Grace."

"Thanks! You too."

I finish the bottle.

4:00 am

My stomach wakes me. Knives. Axes. Fists. Clench. Gag. Clench. Time passes. The storm settles. I observe my surroundings. I'm on the couch. I'm sitting straight up. The usual. The TV is on, empty bottles surround me. I turn the TV off, pick up the bottles. I put the empties away. I stumble to the bathroom. I shower. I get out of the shower. I don't know why I showered. I dry off. I go to bed. I continue my pass-out.

11/29/07, Crush

Grace and I have been texting lately and talking a bit on *Facebook*. We don't talk over the phone. I hate the phone. Our schedules don't mesh during the day. I drink at night. The phone can potentially blow my cover. I text her. She's sweet. Her heart is warm, her confidence is attractive, and her goals are admirable. I told her to study hard for her final exams and I'll take her for a celebratory dinner when she finishes. That's not for a few weeks. I'm prolonging it, so I can fix myself. It's enough time to clean up my act. But not tonight. It's Thursday. It's basically the weekend. I'll drink tomorrow, so why hold off tonight? Persuasive delusional logic.

11/30/07, Session Four: Playing with Pain

9:00 am

I'm becoming overly accustomed to these appointments. I walked straight into Handman's office without the receptionist telling me to do so. His door wasn't fully shut. I walked in. Handman was on the phone.

"Try to stay calm. If you are having these dangerous thoughts—" He turned to see me standing there.

"Sorry," I whisper, as I take the walk of shame back to the waiting room.

After a few minutes the receptionist tells me I can go in. She makes sure to give me a look that says I deserve a time out. She's been bitter toward me since day one. I don't care for her attitude. I make sure she knows. I return a glare from my dark spec less eyes. She looks down. I get to Handman's door and make sure to knock. I walk in.

"Sorry about that. I figured since it was five minutes after, I could come right in." I'm a stickler for time.

"No problem," he says, while writing in his notes.

"Sounded serious. I hope it turns out okay." I sit in the black leather.

"It will. So, Luke, I was thinking we would continue where we left off from last time. Would you like to tell me more about the impact basketball had on your life?"

"I can do that." I reach for my tea. Where's my tea? I forgot to get tea. "Where did we leave off?"

"You were talking about that award you received."

"Right, right. Well, after that camp, I started to play ball whenever I could. I started walking around my block, dribbling the ball through my legs, shooting free-throw shots till I made ten in a row, and all that. I joined a community league, Knights of Columbus. Dave and I were on the same team, with Dad as our coach. I remember one of my first seasons, Dave and I led our team to an undefeated season. I started to attend the U of A camps yearly, receiving all-star, free-throw champ, and three-point-champ type of awards, but nothing like the first. In grade eight, I was the captain of our team. Grade nines were usually captain. It's not saying much, since we were brutal. It was a French school, what do you expect?"

We chuckle.

"After that year, I was awarded a spot on the all-star team. Being the youngest out there and getting the most points was a highlight. After that game, I got asked to go play for another school. At one point, I was playing rep ball, community league, and junior high ball. My second year in rep, I was one of two remaining players. We didn't start out so well. We started in the D squad but worked our way up to B and won the championship. After grade nine, and another all-star game appearance with a new school, I was asked to play football for a high school. Unfortunately, I had to decline. Also in high school, I got asked, almost begged, to play on the school's rugby team. I wanted to but wasn't able to play those sports. Unless I wanted a visit to the hospital."

"Why did they ask you to play football and rugby?"

"Because I was aggressive on the court. They saw my competitiveness and drive. When pain isn't something you worry about, sports are easy to adapt to. No fear, mixed with heart and coordination, goes a long way in sport."

"Interesting. Continue, please."

"Sure thing. Around the time of the all-star game I was asked to try out for the Team Alberta zone team. I ended up being the last cut. They said I was on the team after the first day of tryouts, but the second day I slipped. I didn't get a wink of sleep the night before the second tryout. I was too excited. Pretty shitty, but no excuses. Then—"

Handman cuts me off.

"How did you manage to do so well when you suffered with eczema? Were you in a lot of pain at this time, or was your skin good enough to play?"

"Easy. Passion. The game grew on me, and I loved it. It became my incentive to wake up in the morning. To wipe my dried-up eyes out of darkness. To wobble to the bath to stretch out my skin so I could move my limbs. As much pain as I was in that morning or afternoon, it didn't matter once I got on the court. I remember days when I woke up feeling helpless. I would be in so much pain that sitting up was unbearable. Stretching my limbs was a chore. Opening my eyes wasn't worth seeing. It became a skill to put on my socks without tearing the skin apart and soaking the sock in blood. But, once I got my gear and headed to the gym, the game became the focal point of my thoughts. I didn't have eczema for the next two hours. I had the court, the ball, the baskets, my teammates, and the opponents. I'm very competitive. I don't care what that game means overall. I want to win and by a lot. I remember having a wet washcloth in my gym bag for when I was on the bench sweaty and itchy. But once I got subbed back in, I was back to being normal." I pause. I realize I have answered an unasked question. "Hmm, maybe that is why I became so focused and fond of basketball. It made me feel normal, if not superior. Being the sick kid and beating all these healthy kids was a great achievement."

"That is a good observation. It's a plausible assumption. Basketball gave you a sense of belonging. Continue please."

My thoughts fast-forward to high school. My body tenses from a vision of a past coach.

"What do you want to hear? My kick-ass achievements through ball and how my love for the game was slowly taken away because of a battle with a coach? How this guy made me feel like a piece of shit, pointing me out in front of the others, only to have me reply with a smart-ass comment because I was sick of his shit? How he cut me halfway through a season because of an attitude problem? How, to this day, I clench my teeth and tighten my fists when I think of that douche bag that should rot in hell! Is that what you want to hear, Handman?" My heart skips a beat. My adrenaline speeds up. I stare into Handman's eyes.

He stares into my eyes. He sees what I see when I look in the mirror. Nothing. He sits back in his chair. He looks at his scribbled notepad. He chooses his words carefully, knowing my state of mind.

"Only if you want to, Luke."

"No, I'm good. We'll save it for next week. Later."

I leave his office abruptly. I'm going to Panther tonight.

12/14/07, First Date

7:00 pm

I'm on my way to St. Albert to pick up Grace. I'm nervous. I hate dates. I arrive at her door a couple minutes late. I ring the doorbell. Her dad answers.

"Strike one," he jokes, as I walk in the doorway. I think he's joking.

"Hello, Mr. Clayton, Mrs. Clayton. I'm Luke." I shake her dad's hand, then her mom's.

"Where are you two going tonight?" her dad asks, with a stern look.

A dad's goal is to put fear in a date's eyes. I don't blame him. I'm taking out his daughter with the intention of having sex with her in the near future. I have many intentions with his daughter. I want to make her happy. I want to make her laugh. I want to take care of her and protect her. I want to be her shoulder for tears. I want to be her friend and companion. I want to give her warmth when she's cold. I want to spoil her, treat her like a princess. But one of those intentions is sex. He knows that. I know that he knows. He knows that I know that he knows. It's awkward.

"A restaurant on Whyte Avenue. I forget the name. I've never been. We'll see how it goes."

Mr. Clayton nods and walks to his couch. Grace walks up the stairs from the basement. She looks amazing, with her long, blond hair flowing over her black sweater and her crystal eyes looking into mine. She's a natural beauty.

"Hey, Luke, sorry, I'm just looking for my keys. I can never find my house keys," she says with a smile.

"Take your time."

I look over to see what her dad's watching. UFC. A perfect in.

"Do you think George St. Pierre will beat Matt Hughes next weekend?" I ask him.

"I hope so."

"Yeah, me too. The guy I'm looking forward to GSP beating is Matt Serra. He's a wimp. He made some comments about GSP being French and how he should give up fighting to eat his cheese and drink his wine."

"Ha ha, that's funny. French people." He shakes his head. Don't tell him you're French.

Grace starts walking toward me, waving her house keys excitedly.

"Found them!"

I smile.

"I'm ready when you are," Grace says, as she puts on her shoes.

"It was nice meeting you folks."

"Have fun tonight, you two," her mom says with a smile, while her dad nods and directs his attention back to the fights. I like her parents. Her mom is sweet; her dad is tough. I like that.

We walk out into the brisk air. I made sure to clean Jimmy to the hilt before this date. Some dates I don't bother. This girl is an exception.

"Wow! Your car is really clean," Grace says, acknowledging my hard work.

"Really? Thanks." I shrug and smile.

We continue our small chat throughout the drive. It's initially awkward. We've only previously talked drunk or through text. After a few minutes, the vibe becomes more relaxed. It feels as if we've been on this date a few times. We arrive on Whyte Avenue. We walk into the restaurant Dave recommended. As he promised, it's empty, other than a few couples across the room. Well done, Dave. We sit. We order a bottle of wine. We chat about life. I open up about working with kids. She eats it up. After dinner, we walk back to Jimmy. I let my arm loose. I consider holding her hand. I realize I'm not twelve. I put my hand in my pocket. On the ride home, we share some laughs and flirt. Approaching her house, I'm given a pep talk. *Okay, Luke, be a man. You like this girl; she likes you. Give her a kiss.* "What if she isn't a first-date kisser?" *Then you get rejected. Who cares? What the hell? Why is your heart beating faster? You're a chicken.* We reach her driveway. I put Jimmy in park.

"I had a great time tonight, Grace. You're a lot of fun."

"You are too, Luke." She smiles, exposing her pearly whites. "I figured since we only talked through texting, it was going to be really awkward. But I had a great ..." Our eyes meet. *Make your move.* I lean in for a kiss. Our lips connect. I softly put my hand on her cheek, moving a few strands of hair from her eyes. I feel warmth from her soft lips. I hold her tight and slowly let her go.

"Have a great night, Grace. I'll call you in the next while. Sweet dreams, beautiful."

Grace smiles.

"Goodnight, Luke. Thanks for dinner."

I watch her unlock her door with her found keys. This could be the girl. If only I can find a way to stop drinking. How will I hide it from her if it gets serious? What if she finds out? I can't let anyone find out. Paranoia sets in. It's been happening a lot lately. I don't know why. *Alcohol, Luke.* "I hate alcohol. I love alcohol. It makes life easy." *It's ruining you.* "Ahhh, fuck. I know." I put Jimmy in reverse and back out of the driveway. I put Jimmy in drive and I drive. I follow the pressure of my right foot controlling Jimmy's strength. I follow my hand-gripped steering wheel directing Jimmy. I park at a liquor store. I have no control.

12/18/07, Session Five: Isolated Disease

9:00 am

I'm awake. I stare at the ceiling. I drank seventeen ounces last night but didn't pass out. I fell asleep around 6:00 am. Pigeon's mocking coos have woken me up off and on since 6:20 am. I curse pigeon. I get up. The last thing I want to do on no sleep is tell a stranger my issues. I reach for my phone. I dial.

"Yeah, is this Dr. Handman's office?"

"Yes it is; what can I do for you?"

"My name is Luke. I'm a patient of Dr. Handman, and I don't think I'm going to make it to our appointment today."

"Unfortunately, since you haven't given twenty-four hours notice, we can't reimburse your money."

"You're kidding, right?"

"No, that's how it is."

"I haven't slept. I don't feel comfortable driving on no sleep, since it's just as bad as driving drunk."

"I'm sorry, sir, but those are the rules."

"That's horseshit. All right, well, if I hit someone on the way, I blame you." I hang up. People annoy me.

10:00 am

Walking into the waiting room, I look at the receptionist. Her eyes are glued to her computer.

"Dr. Handman is ready to see you," she says softly, making sure to keep her eyes away from mine.

I nod. I walk to his office. I sit down.

45

"Hey, Luke. How are you doing today?"

"Not good. I'm on no sleep, yet, I have to come tell a stranger my problems, or else I'm out a hundred and sixty bucks. I could be better."

"Would you like to continue the session?"

"Yes. I paid for it."

He ignores my tension.

"So, how have you been feeling lately?"

"Nothing's changed."

"Would you like to talk about your basketball coach?"

"No." My fists tighten. My teeth clench.

We sit in silence. I try to relax. *You're paying him to help you. Tell him about your drinking. He can't tell anyone.*

"Want to know something?"

Dr. Handman sits up in his chair. He senses progress.

"Yes."

I pause. I sense doubt.

"I uh …" Shit. Find a topic. "My parents are getting a divorce." That should eat some time. *You're pathetic.*

"I'm sorry to hear that, Luke."

"Yeah, it's pretty messed up. It's starting to get heated. They've been calling me, pretty upset with each other. They have asked if I can be the mediator to save their friendship, so they don't have to get lawyers involved."

"That's a lot for you to take on yourself."

"So was taking care of me as a sick kid. Its family; I don't have another option. I need to do this. My brother is going to Thailand for five months, so it's up to me."

"How has their separation affected you?"

I look at him funny.

"Like rainbows and sunshine. What do you think?"

He pauses. Classic shrink move.

"All right, I'll talk." I pause to think how to start. "Dad sat us down in late August. Mom was living in Montreal. At that point, I just figured they travelled a lot, and Mom wanted to go back to her roots for a bit. I didn't think it was serious, and I didn't think about it." Her name is vodka. "Dad told us the divorce was official and that they have agreed to start seeing other people. I got mad and went home." Got shitfaced. "That was a couple of months ago. It's better now—well, between me and Mom, and me and Dad. But they're still battling. Mom just moved back to St. Albert, which makes me relieved and happy. If she needs us, we're close, and if we need her, she's close. She said she was sick of running away from the issue and wanted to be back with her boys, me and Dave. Not to mention all her friends. She needs her kids. She misses us. We miss her." I pause. I'm not feeling it. "And I think we're done on that subject for the day."

"Are you sure?"

"Yes."

"Okay, Luke. Well, we still have some time left. Is there anything you want to talk about?"

"You know what, there is." I reach into my pocket, take out a paper, unfold it, and hand it to Dr. Handman. "I asked my physician awhile ago if I could make a copy of my file, because I'm doing some writing and figuring some things out by tracing my tracks. Here's one page out of a couple hundred." I look at a fold in the paper. I want to unfold it. I shake my head. I look up at Handman. He looks interested.

"Would you like me to read this right now?"

"Go for it. The highlighted area provides the gist. It'll give you a better perspective of my past." I read his book titles on the shelf.

This is the excerpt he reads:

University of Alberta Hospital. Admission Date: January 7, 1997. Discharge Date: January 13, 1997. Date of Birth: February 26, 1985. Luke is an 11-year-old who was admitted to the hospital with severe eczema for in-hospital management of his eczema. The eczema is becoming a significant problem for Luke. It resulted in severe pain, itching, and possibly depression. He is avoiding going to school. He is saying that he feels suicidal and has voiced this several times. He was seen by multiple dermatologists, and he was being managed by his family doctor. Multiple medications have been tried in the past. The parents are overwhelmed and feel guilty and are having difficulty living with him. They actually contemplated moving out of the city, but they are not sure even that will help. Physical Examination: The most prominent finding is lesions of excoriation, dryness, and scaling involving the back of the knees, the back of his upper thighs, between the fingers, and aspects of the elbow and most of his body. Discharge: I think Luke is now in much better condition. Mom is much more comfortable dealing with his eczema; she understands now that it's a chronic problem that will not likely clear, but we can keep it under control. Luke's emotion has improved with the improvement of the eczema. He was attending school in the hospital, and I am hoping that he will go back to his regular school. I will keep the mom in touch with the new research if it is faxed to me from the United States. Thank you for allowing me to participate in the care of this child. Sincerely, a good doctor.

I read Handman's body language. His eyes have widened in shock. His expression is one of empathy.

"Luke, I don't know what to say."

"What is there to say? It's my pain and my family's emotional struggle with it. What hurt was reading about the impact it had on my family. The suicide bit was an obvious cry for help. I never remember voicing it. Like you said when you first met me, I was an optimistic kid. But I think that was the darkest of days. I just never thought I was open about it. It's not something I would normally do. I think I spoke up because I thought about it so much, at that point, that, if I didn't say something soon, something bad would have happened. I knew I thought about it, but it was only so I could eliminate the burden I had caused to the people close to me. I never went so far as to plan my death. The description the doctor gave of my skin isn't enough to paint a picture. You have to imagine all the creases on your body covered with dried scabs itching to be open to bleed. Now imagine having to be the new kid at school on various occasions."

"How often were you the new kid?"

"Umm. In grade six. I went from old school in grade five, to being home-schooled at the end of grade five, to new school in grade six. I knew one buddy who helped me blend in. That year I was hospitalized. Although I had to walk around in pyjama pants and slippers, because pants and shoes hurt my skin and didn't let it breathe, I was well liked. And it showed when my fellow students came to visit me in the hospital. In grade seven I was a new kid, like the rest of grade sevens going into junior high. I blended in well. In grade nine I went from French to English school, because I had a hard enough time learning science, let alone in French. Again, I knew a buddy, this time my best bud, Matt. And again, I blended in well. At this time, my skin was decent enough to hide. I was a new kid along with all the other kids in grade ten making my way to high school. I then went to boarding school halfway through grade eleven, where I managed to hide it well again."

"You mention hiding your eczema a lot. Were you embarrassed or teased?"

"A little bit of both. In grade four, I had a personal bully. He would call me disease boy, eczema boy, red face, original stuff like that. I hated him when I was growing up. Hated him. He was in grade six and big. I always had a grudge against him till one day a couple of years ago. I was working at the casino as a blackjack dealer. He came in one night, wearing a tough-guys-wear-pink pink shirt, really drunk, sat down at my table, and started slurring and annoying everyone at the table. The pit boss gave him a warning, but I wanted to play him. I wanted his money. I usually want the customer to win; that way I get tips. But this wasn't a customer to me. It was him versus me, and I cleaned up. After he lost a couple of hundred, he left. Then, after my shift, I went to a local pub to see this girl. As we were leaving the parking lot, we saw him about to get into a fight. He got beat up by some guy, and his pink shirt was covered in red. I walked away that night with a big smile, and I no longer held a grudge.

"I also got picked on during the early years. I remember, just because I put it in my journal. Apparently, I beat up a couple of kids one time. In my entry, I say several, but I'm sure it was an exaggeration. I usually didn't have too much of a problem with bullies. I was the nice kid, so people were nice to me. When I was a new kid, in grade six for example, I made note of my condition immediately. That year

I got up in front of the class and let them know what the deal was. I told them about my condition and suggested if people asked them about it to tell them it wasn't a big deal and not to worry about it. I told them it wasn't contagious and that it is what it is. That year was easy, because I opened up about it."

"Good for you."

"Thanks."

"Well, I think that about wraps up our hour. Thanks for bringing in that doctor's note."

"No problem. I really want answers."

He nods. We stand. He gives me a pat on the back.

"Take care of yourself, Luke."

"You got it. See ya." I leave.

I walk to Jimmy. Handman's a good man. He gets me to talk. He's professional. I can trust him. Is it enough to get me to spill the truth? Or is he going to tell me to go to AA like I'm some sort of alcoholic? This is a temporary problem. *No, it's not, Luke.* "Fuck off. It's temporary."

4:30 pm

"Hey Luke! Come to the bar with my friends and me," Grace says excitedly over the phone.

"What's the occasion?" It has no relevance to my attendance. I'm going regardless.

"We just finished exams, silly. It's time to party!" We had gone on our date last Friday after her final exam. "Come party with us, Luke."

"Sure. What bar you girls thinking?"

"I think the Branch. Get your friends to come out. We'll pick you up at ten."

"Sounds good."

"See you soon."

"I'm looking forward to it. See ya, Grace." I hang up.

10:00 pm

I'm having a few beers before I go out. No vodka. I'm drinking enough beers to get me tipsy but still coherent. The guys are going to meet us at the Branch.

My leg vibrates. I grab my phone from my jeans pocket.

"Hey, Luke! It's Grace." She sounds a bit tipsy herself. "We're just about at your apartment."

"I'll be down in a bit." I hang up. I grab my coat and keys. I take the elevator and walk into the below-zero Canadian chill. I spot Christy's red Pontiac. I open the car door and get in beside Grace.

"Hey, girls."

"Hey, Luke," they say together. I look at Grace and give her a smile.

She smiles back, leaning closer to me.

"Are your buddies at the bar?"

"They should be," I say as I pull out my phone. I call Matt. They're stuck in a big line outside. "It doesn't sound like they're getting in," I say, satisfied knowing I'm alone with all these ladies. "Sorry about that, girls. You would have liked my friends," I apologize.

"No problem. I'm sure we'll party with them someday. How about we go somewhere on Whyte Avenue," Christy suggests.

"Yeah! Luke you live here. What bar should we go to?" Alexi asks.

"Squirrels isn't bad. Usually doesn't have a big line."

"Are you sure you don't want to meet up with your friends?" Grace whispers in my ear.

"They're big boys. They can survive without me," I whisper back.

We get into Squirrels. I order a round of drinks for the girls. I only buy drinks if I want to date a girl. For the next couple of hours, Grace and I sit at a table, talking. Her friends interject now and again. Our legs touch throughout the night; it's like grade-school footsies.

"Grace, I think we're ready to get going," Christy says, trying not to bother us.

"Okay, that's fine. I'll just stay here with Luke," Grace says, staring into my eyes.

"Okay. Luke, are you going to take good care of my friend here?"

"Of course. We're going to have a great time." I say this while staring into Grace's eyes, itching for the girls to leave.

Grace and I have a few more drinks. We talk, we laugh, we flirt. We leave the bar together, walking along Whyte Avenue to my apartment. Strong winds chill through our bodies. I take off my coat and wrap it around her shivering shoulders. I put my arm around her, sharing my warmth. We get to my apartment, shake off the snow we dragged along, and grab the elevator. We walk into the elevator together. I look at Grace. She looks nervous, excited, and happy. Grace looks at me. Our eyes meet. She smiles. I smile. Beautiful silence. I lean toward Grace for a kiss. The kiss turns into passion, leading us to the bedroom. Before we sleep, I kiss Grace. She kisses me. She wraps herself in my arms. I hold her and rub her back. She falls asleep in my arms. I stare at the ceiling. I think I found her. I look down at Grace. She's calm and peaceful. I'm met with fear. I haven't fixed my burden. I promised myself I would before anything happened. I have to heal myself. I will heal myself. I want to be with her. She's my incentive. *You're wrong, Luke. It doesn't work that way.* "Yes, it does. I control my destiny." I look down at Grace. I imagine myself spoiling her and making her the happiest girl alive. I pass out.

12/24/07, Christmas Eve

I finally got this right. Dave and I are going to Mom's for Christmas Eve and morning. We're still going to Mass, but without Dad. Then, after we open presents at Mom's in the morning, we'll go to Dad's to open presents. And then we'll go to the Tougas Christmas dinner with Dad but not Mom. Separations are confusing.

3:55 pm

I park Jimmy next to a Mercedes and a Beamer. Typical vehicles for this crowd. I'm meeting Mom, Dave, and his new girlfriend at a special Christmas service in Fort Edmonton. A few ex-Edmonton Oilers hockey players—Lowe, MacTavish, Simpson, and Buchberger—attend this Mass, too. I like to talk to the ex-Oilers, and I like that I'm designated bartender at the saloon post-mass. I stick to the one-for-you-two-for-me rule. This year I drove, so I'll have to wait till later. I've been drunk every Christmas Eve since I was thirteen. I hid it till I was eighteen. I still wait for everyone to sleep before I get pass-out drunk. I hate living a lie. I walk into the church. I'm late. We don't get a chance to say our hellos. During the sermon and the time for the "peace be with you," I text Grace: "Peace be with you." I don't take church seriously. With a few minutes left in the service, I slip out to go prepare the bar. Before everyone gets there, I down a couple of shots, soothing my body. The bartending goes smoothly. Mac T, who now coaches the Oilers, and Simmer, who now is a sports broadcaster both come up to the bar. We have a chat. They're interested in how school is going. I'm not. I'm interested in the Oilers' potential. I enjoy talking to the pros. When they leave, I reflect on a childhood memory.

My family was staying at my Uncle Richard's cabin. Mac T had a cabin next door. Our families coordinated a time to get together. One night, Dad, Dave, Mac T, Simmer, and I were sitting around the fire. The old men were smoking their cigars and drinking beers. Mac T and Simmer told stories about precise moments of the Stanley Cup Finals in the eighties. I was on the edge of my seat. Later in the night, they challenged me to swim in the lake for twenty bucks. Before they could reconsider, I stripped down to my boxers. I bolted toward the below-zero water. I swam to the end of the dock. My nuts pruned. Good times.

I shake away the cloud of memories. Someone's asking for a Bailey's and coffee. I remind her Bailey's won't do the trick. She laughs. I was serious. I serve more drinks. I eat a few snacks. I grab my keys. I had two shots within three hours. I drive to Mom's to meet everyone. I walk into Mom's new pad to find my mother, Lucie, cheerful, as always.

"Son!" She gives me a big hug and a kiss on each cheek. "How are you, my handsome baby?"

I love this lady. Her life's a battle, but she's the happiest one around. I know she hurts inside right now, but her optimism and strength give me strength.

"Great, Mom. How are you? How are you settling in?" I ask, looking down.

Lucie is petite. Her brown eyes, brown hair, tanned skin, great complexion, strong cheekbones, and pearly whites make her a vision of beauty. Her smile lights up rooms. Her eyes sparkle with joy. Growing up, all my friends annoyed the hell out of me with their teenage crushes. Her entrance brings all eyes to her. Her beauty is so deep—it begins with her warm heart.

"Just great. Come in, come in. Your brother is in the kitchen with Chrystal." Chrystal is Dave's new girlfriend. We haven't had a chance to meet.

"Hey, shitbrick," Dave greets me kindly.

Dave is two years older than me. He resembles the actor James Franco. Dave thinks it's the other way around, but I make sure to remind him that James Franco has no clue that he exists. When

Mr. Franco comes out with a new film, Dave gets more girls. He was teased about his size when he was growing up, and now those guys steam when they see Dave with another gorgeous girl. The ugly duckling wins again.

"Hey, shithead."

"Hey, you two!" Mom peeps up. "There is a lady here." She points to Chrystal.

I turn around. Sexy girl. Tall, brunette, with piercing blue eyes. I look at Dave. I give him a congratulatory nudge. I walk toward Chrystal.

"Hey, Chrystal, I'm Luke." I lean in to shake her hand.

"The ugly one of us." Typical Dave.

Chrystal laughs. "Hey, Luke, nice to meet you." We shake hands, sharing a smile.

I turn back to Mom. "So, when's dinner?" I rub my stomach. There's a deep silence in the room. Chrystal, Dave, and Mom look at each other and burst into laughter.

"What's going on?" I scratch my head. I'm confused.

"Ha ha, um, I don't think we're having turkey anytime soon," Mom tries to explain. "I don't think this oven works. The turkey has been in there for hours and is still pretty raw." She's embarrassed. A rare occasion for her.

"Good, I don't want turkey. Let's order Chinese." We've been ordering Chinese food every Christmas Eve since we watched *The Christmas Story* a couple of decades ago. It has become a tradition. But then, so was spending Christmas Eve with the whole family.

"Great idea." Mom's relieved.

"Chinese food?" Chrystal's confused.

"It's the only delivery service open Christmas Eve. No Jesus's birth for Asians," I educate.

Chrystal smiles. She thinks we're crazy, or she digs the idea. We order Chinese food. We eat and share many laughs. Later in the evening, we watch home videos. It proves Dave is adopted. We're nothing alike. He was a skinny, out-of-control-in-need-of-Ritalin brat. I was a chubby, quiet, sick momma's boy. I look like Dad, so I can't be the adopted one. I wasn't expecting such a great night. I wish

Dad could be here to share laughs with us. After Chrystal goes home and Mom goes to bed, Dave and I play Wii. We have some beers. We have a serious chat about Mom and Dad. He has been living at Mom's the past month. He sold his place in Edmonton and is going to Thailand for five months. He has been with Mom through the tension of the separation. It's good Mom has him around. I haven't done much, knowing I have to take over when he leaves in early January. He gives me a few heads-ups and pointers.

Later, Dave goes to sleep on the couch. I called the guest bedroom. He had called it first. When we were younger, and he was bigger, and I was a gimp, I would call something, and he would say, "I'll fight you for it." I pulled that one on him tonight. I'm at least thirty pounds heavier and a couple of inches taller now. I get the bed, even though it's his room when he stays here. Karma. When I sense Dave's asleep, I go to my overnight bag and pull out a bottle of vodka. I sit on the bed, staring out the window at the naked sky. I chug. I've always been the last one up. Ever since I can remember. Insomnia fucks with my head. I'm awake when people sleep. I sleep when people are awake. People think I sleep in, because, by the time I fall asleep, I need to sleep longer than others to get in a few hours. Does that mean everyone that goes to bed before 3:00 am goes to bed early? I can wake up at noon on four hours of sleep. That's not sleeping in. People don't get it. They can't, unless they experience insomnia themselves. People expect people to be like themselves. That's ignorance—the opposite of acceptance. No one person is the same. We can't be. If we were, that would be a fucked-up world. Darkness gives me weird thoughts. I picture the world of a single identity. I feel a deep sleep coming. I hope Santa brings me a new liver.

12/26/07, Boxing Day

For Christmas Dad got us the coolest gift. We're going to Denver to watch NFL and NHL games. Dad has a hookup through his travel agent, who knows the owner of the Denver Broncos. One morning we will tour the Broncos training facilities, and then we will watch a Colorado Avalanche game. The next day, we will stand on the sidelines during practice before the Broncos' last game of the season. Then, after the game, we can go back out onto the field. I'm pumped! I've never been to an NFL game. It's my favourite sports league.

I'm on the airplane home. That was amazing. Unfortunately, I got so shitfaced every night that my days were spent hung over. One blackout night, I got so drunk that I started to wrestle Dave and cut my head against the bed frame, filling a washcloth full of blood. I then passed out halfway off the bed, clinging to the wall to support me in my sleep. Dave took a picture to rub in my idiocy.

But I'll never forget that NFL game. It did nothing for the Broncos, because they were already out of playoff contention. But it went into overtime, and they won. It was a great game. I got a picture with Brendan Stockley. He was my favourite receiver when he played for the Colts. I became an NFL fan when I was eighteen. Before then, I would watch the Edmonton Eskimos every week during football season with Dad and Dave. When I was about fifteen, Dave introduced me to the NFL. I liked the CFL better, during that year, because I had my home town to cheer for. But as I watched the next couple of NFL seasons, I was in awe. These guys pummelled each other. They made the most miraculous game-winning/saving drives/plays/catches/passes/interceptions. You name it, the NFL has it. It's the greatest franchise to hit sport. It's the most complicated and most intense. After watching games on Sundays, Mondays and, later, Thursdays for a couple of seasons, I decided to pick a team to cheer for. I made my choice at Dave's one day. I reflect back to that day.

We were watching a Colts/Redskins game. At this point, I was deliberating between the San Diego Chargers and the Indianapolis Colts. I liked the Chargers, because LT has wicked initials, and he's very elusive and exciting to watch. But, on the Colts side, I enjoyed watching them from both positions: defence and offence. Freeney and Mathis on the defensive ends crushed quarterbacks and running backs in unison. Bob Sanders, as a corner, took out receivers mid-stride. On the offensive end, it was exciting and interesting to watch and observe the clutch, intellect, and poise of Manning and his receiver duo, Harrison and Wayne. I basically knew I was a Colts fan, but I let Dave make that official. We were watching the game. Manning had just taken the Colts to another last-minute drive victory to beat Dave's team. Dave looked disgusted and mumbled, "I hate Manning."

I nodded. A smile appeared on my face. The rivalry was born. "I love the Colts. Peyton is amazing. Go, Colts!"

That year, they lost the first round in the playoffs to the Chargers, but they won the '06 season! The Colts took out Rex "Wreck" Grossman and the Bears.

5:00 pm

I'm home. Grace is on her way over before she goes to work. We're not dating yet. She isn't sure she's ready to start dating, because she wants to make sure that this time it's the right choice. I haven't fixed my burden. I'm not the right choice. I am the right choice. When we date, I'll fix my burden. I'm becoming negative toward the situation. I have to ease up. I don't want her to sense my hidden misery. She would know I'm not the right choice. For now, we hang out. I'll charm her and make up for a drunken call I don't remember making to her in Denver. Then I'm off to St. Albert to get shitfaced. It's New Year's. All the cool kids are doing it.

Grace and I are official. I had her over for dinner. I impressed her with my cooking skills. We had some wine. I gave her a candlelight massage. In bed, before we went to sleep, I told her I would love to brag that she's my girlfriend. She smiled and said she would like that. I guess I'm the right choice. *Don't bring anyone into this misery.* "Love will conquer all." *Not in your state.* "You were on my side before." *But now I see you are hopeless. I read your thoughts. You will never quit.* "When I fall in love, I'll quit." *You'll break this girl's heart.* "No. I'll fall in love, quit drinking alone, and treat her like gold." *Not how it works. You read about it every day. You know this, Luke.* "Stop fighting me on this. It's all I have left."

01/14/08, Session Six: Masked Identity

6:00 am

Silence.

"Coo, coo."

I punch the window. The blinds dent. Calm. Storm. Stomach. Knives. Axes. Punches. Bathroom. Puke. Bile. Bed. Defeat. I stare at the ceiling. I ride out the second wave. An hour passes. I get up. I go for a swim. I get some research and work papers done. I feel like shit. I try to meditate. No go. I try to eat. No go. I go to the bathroom and take a whiz. I look in the mirror. My dark hair's matted, my eyes rest over bags, my skin tone's pale. I look like shit. *You're the biggest nobody I've ever seen. Just doing what your dead uncle did, hey, big shot?* "Don't remind me of my uncle. He's dead. Get over it." *And so will you be if you keep it up.* "He lasted till he was forty-six. I have lots of life left." *You're losing it, Luke.* "How do I lose you?" *Stop drinking.*

10:00 am

Although I feel worse than most days, I'm going to put on a happy mask till I get home to my secluded capsule. Today is the perfect day to repair damage. I haven't seen Handman for awhile because of Christmas holidays. The time is perfect to show false progress. It might sound odd for me to hide my identity, but this is typical for me. If I let out too much negativity, I portray a mask of happiness so I don't lead them on to my misery. Mom unknowingly taught me how to hide weakness. When you live a lie, it's part of the job. If I do get caught, I become a burden on others' lives. I'll stick with

62

the happy front. My words are full of optimism and joy. My mind is depressed and angry.

I search for my mask. I leave my apartment. I ignite Jimmy. I drive. I park Jimmy. I walk to the building. I get off the elevator. I stop at the door. I collect myself. I take a few deep breaths. I put on my mask. I open the door. I walk in with a smile.

"Oh, hey, you're looking lovely today," I say cheerfully to the receptionist.

"Oh." She seems a little shocked. "Thank you," she replies with a careful smile.

You really haven't been nice to this one, have you? She's scared of your kindness. Time for damage control.

"I want to apologize for my negative attitude toward you lately. I have had a rough month of sleep. It's why I'm here." I let out a smile-slash-chuckle, hoping for a pity laugh.

"Oh, ha ha, that's okay. It's part of the job."

"I bet. But that is no excuse for me to take my issues out on you. I apologize." I say this staring at her eyes. I wait for eye contact to show her "true" sincerity.

Our eyes connect. She's at ease.

"That is very nice of you. Dr. Handman is ready to see you in his office, Luke."

"Thank you. Take care." People annoy me.

I walk into Handman's office with an extra boost to my step.

"Dr. Handman. What is going on, my friend?" I say, smiling from ear to ear.

"Hey, Luke." He looks at me with an expression I can't identify. He's happy that I seem happy, or he's hiding his doubt. I hope it's the former. Today is all about spreading smiles and happiness. I want to puke.

"You seem to be in better spirits."

"Well, of course, it's a beautiful day. Life is good." I think I might puke. "Dr. Handman, where is the bathroom? I drank too much water this morning." I smile.

"Just outside the office, go down the hall, second door to your left."

"Thanks."

I walk to the bathroom. I lean against the wall. I dry heave. I get cold sweats. My stomach punches me. My intestines shred. I drag myself to the sink. I splash my face with water. I give my head a shake. I stare at the mirror and tell myself to suck it up. I put my mask back on. I walk back to his office. I sit down.

"So, what should we talk about today, doc?"

"Well, Luke. We have been talking about your past. You have had a very difficult start to your life. A lot in your life has been taken from you, and you went through lots of personal struggle, but what I am interested in is how you are today. You seem to be a strong, intelligent man but still a little broken. How about we talk about yourself today and your future goals?"

My goals and ambitions are a joke to me. I know who I am. I know what I am. I don't know *why* I am who and what I am. My goals are unreachable. I'll speak the truth of what I want. But it's a lie. It won't happen.

"Well, when I was twelve, during my dark days of suicidal ideations, I saw this child psychologist who helped me gain an understanding of my existence. After that specific session, I did some soul searching. In our grade-five class, we were asked to write down what we wanted to be when we grew up. I wrote that I wanted to be a professional basketball player, like all child athletes with pro ambitions. Underneath that, I wrote if that wasn't going to happen then I wanted to be a child psychologist. I completely misspelled psychologist. My parents kept that assignment, knowing my ambitions. And till about a year ago, this was significant. I wanted to go to school, get my doctorate, and work with kids. But when I was in youth intervention, working with kids in group, foster, and broken homes, I didn't think it was for me. I excelled at what I did, and the kids looked up to me. But after a year and a half and a large amount of exposure, I gave up. I felt torn at that time. I felt I wasn't strong enough to do what I wanted to do." A jolt of pain hits my stomach. I straighten up. I hide weakness. "I worked with kids from the ages of eight-to seventeen-years-old. My job was to show them their capabilities and to pinpoint to them what they excelled at and to help them focus on their dreams. Some I worked with for a few months or half a year, and there were three siblings I worked with since I started. The last half year before I left, those siblings were split up into separate foster homes all over Edmonton and area, and the only time they saw each other was when I picked them up to spend the Sunday with them. They were NFL fun-loving Sundays, mind you."

Dr. Handman smiles.

"We would spend really great days and some tough days where we all, in the end, pulled through. The two brothers and sister were on good terms, and life was good. But behind those scenes emerged a display of politics. I had an argument with a foster mom who was pressing religion on one of the kids. She called me a crazy atheist, because I said I didn't believe all Catholics or Christians, whatever it is, show an open casket at funerals and that I have been to a few funerals and never seen that. Before this argument, all I told the teen was that I didn't believe it, and she didn't have to either. She was uncomfortable with the thought, so I told her not to worry about it. Being excited about having choices in life, she expressed this to her new foster mom. This is when her foster mom called me, flipped out, and went into her little rant. I told her I was doing her a favour for free, so she should cool it. This is when she decided to pull out the atheist crap. I was pissed. I considered running my mouth, but instead I hung up. I called my supervisors before I retaliated and said that foster mom is reaching the limit. Later the girl told me she only told her foster mom that she liked the thought of not having to see dead people. She had heard the conversation on the phone and felt bad. I told her she had nothing to do with it. Stupid religion. This lady had been her foster mom for a month and was already brainwashing her. Her house was filled with religious propaganda. It completely eliminated individual thought." I swallow. My stomach curdles.

"Then this other kid I was working with got hit by a train. He heard voices, due to untreated schizophrenia, because he stopped taking his meds. He was sent to the psych ward, and later busted out. Five days later, they found him dead. At the funeral, with a couple dozen friends and family of Tiger, I went up and talked and made sure to mention who Tiger talked about on a weekly basis: his friends and the positive impact they had on him to start training to go to the army and helping him with his talent in rap lyrics. He was always a positive kid, with lots of ambition."

I miss you, Tiger. I learned a lot from you. I'll always wish they had let me come see you. We could have done something. I know it. I miss you, dude. I wish we could still hang out—walk around Whyte Avenue, get some Greek food, go to an Internet cafe, listen to your rap, read your inspiring lyrics, window shop, and talk about life. I miss our laughs, man. I'll never forget you.

Handman sees I'm deep in thought. I haven't blinked.

"So, yeah, to break it down, I couldn't deal with it anymore. I'll always miss the kids and wish them the best. I know what each and every one of them has the potential to be. I hope one day a guy with a love for old-fashioned cars, who has fetal alcohol spectrum disorder, will be fixing my car, because he will be the best mechanic around. Of course, as you know, you can't come into contact with clients after you quit. A couple of them have tried to call or add me on *Facebook*, and I must notify my past employer, without responding. It hurts. They only want to talk because they trust me. A couple of them left messages on my phone saying they couldn't believe I'd left. They weren't angry. They were sad, which is worse. Resentment is easier than pain. I did that to them. I did that to myself." I pause. I sigh.

Handman nods. He gives the shrink pause. He reads me.

I feel pain. Not physical. I feel weakness rising. I close my eyes. I gather strength. I keep my mask on. I push the weakness down. I breathe.

"So, then I considered sports psychology. But after talking to a friend, Craig MacTavish, the head coach of the Edmonton Oilers, I learned that their sports psychologist, like most sports psychologists, is hired only on a part-time basis. So, at this point, I didn't know what I wanted to be. That was about six months ago. Then I came across an internship program in psychology at school. I sat down with the advisor in charge and went through the job listings. Out of the forty or so options, only one had caught my eye. It was a job teaching kids with autism. Earlier I had read a book called *The Curious Incident of the Dog in the Night-time,* by Mark Haddon, about this child with Asperger's, a mild form of autism. Before I read this novel, I hadn't known anything about autism. I had so many unanswered questions after reading the book that I wanted to learn more. This child fascinated me. I told my advisor that was the job I wanted—and that's the job I got. And I excel at it. I love what I do. These kids are my life, and I have a lot to offer them. I still want to get my doctorate ..." The unreachable part. "... and work with families of kids with autism. I also want to write a book about my childhood, so I can get awareness for eczema. I also plan to start a charity foundation for eczema and one for autism. I want to make a huge difference in this fucked-up world." I tense up. Oh shit. A slip. Clean it up. "Well, that's how I felt as a child. Sorry if that sounded harsh. It just came back to me. But it's good, because it reminds me where I am today and why I'm doing what I'm doing."

Dr. Handman leans back in his chair. He's confused. He tries to read into what I just said. He reads my body language.

I attempt to cut off his thoughts.

"So, basically, I still want to be a psychologist. Do you think I have the qualifications? I remember a professor at school saying that the best shrinks are the ones who had a tough start in life, because they can relate to hardship and personal struggle. That put me at ease. What do you think?" Does he know what I'm doing?

"Yeah, for sure, Luke. I believe you are an intelligent man who's going through a rough patch with strength and courage. Once we can find happiness within you, I believe you will be a great psychologist. But, to be honest, I don't believe you feel as good as you're professing today. Why is that?"

He's good. Not only did he see through your front, but he redirected your redirected question back to his initial inkling. Well played, Handman. I have options.

"What do you mean? I had a great morning." I tense up. I fake it. "I finally feel good about myself, and you're accusing me of displaying a false character. I'm paying you, so why wouldn't I be honest?" Awareness of my deceit tightens my muscles. I'm aware. I know what I'm doing. I know it's wrong. My tension becomes real. *You're an idiot. He's giving you nothing but opportunities.*

Handman's put off-guard. Have I changed his mind or just made him uncomfortable to make any more observations?

"Well ... Luke ... I mean, I'm not, I mean—"

"Don't bother. I think time's up anyway. I need some food. You're a smart man, but maybe I'm not the right client for you. Maybe I'm not ready for help." I pause. I consider giving up. "But I'll be back, because you are smarter than most." I indirectly told him he was right. "I'm not saying you're right, but I do acknowledge your guts. See ya." I get up. We shake hands.

He looks distraught.

I'm distraught.

I walk to Jimmy. I'm concerned. What just happened? Did someone see through me? "Clean it up, Luke," I tell myself, "or you slip, get busted, and no drinking for life." *Luke, you need to get busted.* "I can fix this."

01/22/08, Session Seven: Desperate for Answers

My eyes open. I'm surrounded by darkness. Knives strike my intestines. Axes swing through my gut. Fists pummel my stomach. "Fuck." I sit up. I'm on the couch. I look around. An empty mickey bottle lies on the coffee table. A half bottle of wine sits on the counter. I look up at the stove. It's 2:07 am. When did I pass out? I slowly pick myself up. I walk to the kitchen counter. I grab the bottle. I gag. I chug. I finish the bottle. I go to the bathroom. I brush my teeth in darkness. I walk to my bedroom. I pass out.

9:30 am

"Coo, coo."

Of course. I walk out of my room to the balcony doors. I softly open the sliding door, with a shoe in hand. I slam it onto the cement a few feet from the pigeon. Bam! The pigeon is off in a hurry. I watch it fly away. It circles. "Fuck. Don't come back." It starts coming back. I rush toward it. Pigeon cuts sharp and is off. I walk back inside. I rub my eyes to clear the blur of numbers on the stove. Pigeon woke me up in time for my appointment. I guess they're not all bad. I turn back toward the balcony. I look down at all the shit from their many visits. Damn pigeons.

10:00 am

I park Jimmy. I haven't seen Handman since he saw through me. I won't lie to him anymore. He can't say a word to anyone of importance in my life. If he does, I sue him and make money. Win/win. Does this mean I'll talk about my drinking? I doubt it. *Your oblivion baffles me.* I walk to Handman's office. I stop midway to get a tea. *Ah, you remembered. You're a genius. It's almost as if you can take care of yourself.* "Shut up!" I tell the back of my mind to shut up. I continue down the hall.

"Take a seat, Luke. I'll be with you in a minute. I'm just finishing up some papers."

"Sure." I text Grace while I wait: "Good morning, gorgeous. How is your day going?"

Then it's back to Handman. "So, Luke. Let's cut to it. If you want my help, I need you to tell me everything you feel and not what you want me to believe you feel." Handman rubs in his victory.

I nod.

"I admire your strength to turn a negative in your life and do something positive with it. I believe you have a strong future ahead of you. But we need to look deeper to the root of the cause of your pain. What is it that seems to be causing conflict within your thoughts? Why haven't you felt better since your skin has gotten better?"

"All right. Well, let's see. I remember always holding resentment toward others who took life for granted. I felt that if I had access to moving limbs without intense pain then I would be king of the world. I felt I would live every moment to its fullest and make a huge impact in this world. Maybe I dreamt too high at a young age, or maybe it's because my mobility never has actually straightened out for good. It's an endless war. I still have to spend a couple of days in bed at times to rest my body, because my skin can quickly take a bad turn." *Drinking doesn't help.* "I remember being a garbage man and asphalt employee for the City of St. Albert, and I was doing fine, but then, after about a month, my skin got so bad that one day I went to work and my boss, who understood my condition, told me that for my benefit I should quit, because it could only get worse. I looked that bad in coveralls." I laugh.

Handman pity-laughs.

I continue.

"I have tried many summers to work for Access Plumbing, my Dad's company, but I could never last longer than a month before having to rest for a few days in bed. It has never really gone away. I'll never know if it's gone for good, because the doctors I have seen in the past said they have never seen a case like mine. They said most people grow out of it, but, in my case, they don't know if I'll ever get rid of eczema. I have to find that out on my own. But what I think is the real issue is not the state of my skin at the moment. I can manage that. It's my memories. When my skin takes a bad turn like that, I am reminded of a trace of pain from when I was an adolescent. And, as much pain as it is for a twenty-two-year-old, it hurts to know that at a younger age I dealt with pain ten times what I am dealing with at the moment. And that hurts—to know how badly children can suffer. Having to deal with so much pain at a young age is an eye opener, and it's a sad taste of reality to know other kids out there suffer worse than I do from a broad spectrum of issues. Having to see pain in the eyes of strangers is something I could do without. Having my stomach turn to knots when I see someone eating alone, because I feel they might not have companionship—even though I myself like to eat alone—I can do without. But I can handle shedding a tear when I see children living in hospitals, having lived in hospitals myself and having suffered a fraction of what they are going through—because that pushes me to succeed. But at the same time, it's all part of my self-destructive path ..." *Another slip.* ".... You know what I mean. That I'm where I should be but feel something is still missing or unsolved. It's the underlying issues from a complicated childhood that creates scars." I pause. The back of my mind wants to talk. *Everything that has happened in your life has happened for a reason. You experience others' pain, so you can be the best one to help them. It's because you see other's pain before yours that you're on this path of self-destruction. You're still torn, because you're drinking away your life and not dealing with your past. But your ambitions are all still attainable. Man, you're oblivious. Wake up.* The back of my mind knows but doesn't acknowledge that I can't see my life without alcohol. It's a useless topic. *You're useless.* "Fuck off! You're driving me insane!" *You're doing this to yourself, Luke.*

"Is something on your mind?"

I look up. Handman looks puzzled. I realize the conversation I was having was in my head.

Oh ... uh ... no, I'm good. Um, yeah ... so, where were

i were making real progress there. You see yourself helping otho. because you can relate to hardship. That is a very positive attitude. And you say that you have your goals in mind, but you're not happy with yourself. I haven't completely understood why yet. I understand you see others' pain before your own, which is good, but you have to put yourself first. But, like you said about underlying issues, well, I think there is one here."

Oh shit.

"What do you mean?" I cross my legs and make a fist under my chin. A mock role reversal.

"Well, there is something that is keeping you from happiness. Maybe it's your parents' separation, or your uncle's death, or the other deaths in your life. Or maybe it's just about talking about your childhood and releasing those repressed memories."

"I'm old enough to understand that divorce is common. According to most of my psychology and sociology books, divorce has a fifty-two percent chance of happening. It sucks of course, because they were the "it" couple—madly in love. From what I saw. And the deaths, well I dealt with them at the funeral..." I don't want to talk about my parents or grieving, so I lie. "...The childhood bit is definitely something I have to work on. I don't know if you're on the right track, but maybe next time we should dig deeper into those issues. See if maybe something comes up."

"Okay Luke, that sounds good. I think we're getting somewhere."

I smile. My mind laughs at me.

"Later Handman." I stand up.

I leave. I'm met with fear. Paranoia traps the back of my mind. *You're dying.* Walking to Jimmy, I try to avoid thoughts. They're too powerful. *Why are you paying to lie to someone, when you know what you need to do?* "Research." *You're really pissing me off.* "I have to get to work. All you're good for is to help me find strategies for these kids." *I'm here to wake you up, before you die.* "I'm young. I have a few years left." *You will die soon.*

My phone vibrates. It's a text from Grace. "Morning, babe. My morning is good. Are you on your way to work?"

I haven't told Grace I'm seeing a shrink. It's a sign of weakness. I look at the time on my phone. It's 12:05 pm. I'll text her back before work.

12: 50 pm

I pull up to work. I grab my phone. "Yeah I'm just getting to work. Movie tonight?"

I go to work.

11: 50 pm

I'm home from dropping Grace off. It was a bad night. I wasn't nice. I got mad about something to do with her ex. It's sick, because I don't remember what. Poor girl. I make shit up. My thoughts don't make sense. Today, I was praised at work by a psychologist who came to see how our program's going. He says it's amazing for these kids to have a guy with such a calm demeanour. He says it helps the kids feed off my patience and relaxes them, which increases positive behaviours. But then I go home, invite my girlfriend over to my place, find something to get angry about, exaggerate it, and work off that for the night. I don't know what I got mad about, and I don't know why. I don't want to fight. I love being with her. I'm falling in love with her. I don't like to fight. We have no reason to fight. My sole purpose is to make her happy. I'm not making her happy. I'm causing doubt and confusion. It's not because she isn't the right one. I've met enough girls to know exactly what I want in a girl. She has the whole package. She likes me so much that she willingly deals with my shit and forgives me when I apologize. This is already becoming a regular occurrence. I dropped her off in time to get to my liquor store before it closed. Time to drink. *Luke, you can't do this to Grace anymore.* "When I tell her I love her, I'll quit drinking alone." *No, you won't.* "Once again, it's all I have left."

6:00 am

I wake up. The calm. It slowly creeps, then hits with a thundering jolt. I grind my teeth and ride it out. I go to the bathroom. I puke. I shit. The pains subside. I go back to bed. I feel the second wave emerging. I lie in bed. I prepare. A knife pierces my intestines. I groan. An axe hits my gut in full swing. I grimace. A lone fist uses my gut as a punching bag. I curse. Pigeon coos. I bang the window. I curse. Pigeon coos. I curse. My stomach shreds. I gag. I get cold sweats. I curse. I fight pain. I lie in defeat. I'm fucked. I ride out the third wave. An hour passes. I stare at the ceiling, motionless, numbed from the pain. I have to go see Handman. I go clean up. The pains follow. I get ready. I grab my mask.

9:00 am

I park Jimmy. I take the elevator. I put on my mask. I walk into Handman's office on time. He's also on schedule. We sit.

"How are you doing today, Luke?"

"I'm feeling a little hungover." *Really?* "It was a friend's birthday last night." It wasn't. *Shithead.*

"Yeah, that will happen."

Dr. Handman's not much of a drinker, which is why I never mention a word of it. Today I did, because one time can't hurt, and it's a hint for him. It's up to him to take what I say and pick up on other subtle hints. Why I have turned this into a game I don't know. It's what my life has turned into. I'm a secret. I'm trapped in a lie, a vicious cycle. I'm in too deep. I've dug four feet into the earth.

Uncle Gary says that at my pace I should dig faster. I do. I want to get busted. I want to tell Grace. I want to tell someone. I want to tell anyone. I'm too ashamed.

"Yeah, I like how I fall asleep right away, or is that what the boozers call a pass-out?" I say with a half chuckle.

He stares at me.

I continue.

"But yeah, I don't feel the best today. I should be good soon. Anyhow, what were you thinking we should talk about?"

I sense he questions digging into what I've said. He hesitates and keeps his thoughts to himself. Wise move.

"Well, I was wondering if you could tell me what an average day was like for you when your skin condition was at its peak of severity."

"I can do that. You do know you're bringing up the most repressed of the repressed memories. I'm going to relive it because I trust you might be able to help me out." I pause. I take a deep breath. "Okay, one of the worst memories was near the end of grade six, so I was about eleven. It was around the time of that U of A hospital admission summary I showed you. After that admission, I ended up back in the hospital. When I was in grade five, I was going to an old, mouldy school, which had been causing harm to my skin and asthma. So, for the last couple of months of school I was home-schooled, and I was to go to a new school in grade six. My skin wasn't getting better during home-schooling, and it only got worse at the new school." I close my eyes and put myself in my bed at eleven years of age.

"This is what a typical day was like. I would wake up to darkness and pain. I would wish I had never woken up. I couldn't see, because pus was dried up around my eyes, gluing them shut. My limbs would be stuck in the fetal position, because prior to falling asleep I would scratch my sores, leaving them open, and they'd dry while I slept. I'd wake up and experience a moment of blindness. I'd search for the warm, wet cloth waiting for me on my bedside table. After carefully dabbing my eyes for a couple of minutes, making sure not to tear them open, I'd adjust to the light, seeing the blurry image surrounding the strings of moistened pus. Once that was done, I'd call for Mom. Mom would walk in, all angelic, with a halo around her head, say 'Good morning, sweetie,' and reach her hand out for me to grab. As I would slowly manoeuvre my body near the edge of the bed, I would put some pressure on her hand, taking her strength to lift myself up."

I give him a display of these actions. "At this point, I'm half bent over, somewhat like a penguin or a ninety-year-old man with arthritis. If I stretch my body, I risk tearing the dried skin over my creases, which is one of the worst pains associated with severe eczema. I'm not talking about one crease. I'm talking about every part of your body where you have ability to move. Those creases. So Mom guides me to my prepared bath. A shower at this time is not an option, because the pressure from the shower head tears apart my skin, leaving a puddle of blood streaming down the drain. Once I get in the bath, I slowly start straightening my limbs. The water moistens my skin, enabling my ability to move. It takes awhile. Once this is done, my mom wraps me up, and I lie in my parents' bed, because they have a TV. Then Mom covers me with whatever cortisone cream my doctor has prescribed at the time, hoping this one will work. None of them do. Mom then has to go wipe off the dead skin covering my bloodstained sheets. Then she washes them.

"My days consisted of lying in bed watching daytime TV with Mom or by myself. I didn't watch soaps. I hate soaps." We laugh. "Or I would do my homework or write in my journal."

"You had a journal?"

"Yeah, I kept my thoughts in there. I've read over them. Like I said, I have been tracing my tracks, trying to answer some questions. Mom gave me a box of stuff I wrote as a kid."

"Interesting. Keep going. Sorry for the interruption."

"No problem. So, basically, I spent the days with Mom. Dave and my friends were at school, and Dad was at work. Mom and I hung out, cooked, watched movies, and went to hospitals and doctors of all kinds. We spent our days together. We enjoyed each other's company. She showed me strength I never imagined someone could have. But, like I said, Handman, it wasn't the pain I personally experienced on a day-to-day basis. It was seeing the pain hidden beneath her eyes. I would lie in bed, helpless, knowing she was looking at my bloodstained sheets and wiping off my dead skin with silent tears. I saw the tension I caused my family. I saw my brother rebelling, to seek attention and love, because I was two full-time jobs."

I stop talking. I become stone.

"Take your time, Luke. Don't feel you have to keep going."

I sit motionless. I stare out the window. I watch people drive and glide the icy roads, surviving another day. Bitter faces walk the streets. A fog over their eyes. A blizzard in their sights. Fear. Struggle. For what? This?

Five minutes pass. I slowly ease up.

"Sorry."

I continue to watch the struggle. Five minutes pass. Expensive silence.

"I hate this part. Here is this attractive young couple, full of aspirations and looking forward to starting a happy, healthy family together. They dream of having lots of kids, around five. But after that second one comes, he becomes nothing but work, because he is in constant need, dependent on others to survive and get through his daily regimens. The picture-perfect family slowly deteriorates. Relationships become a strain, because Luke is so sick. Optimism and happiness fade. The struggle worsens without showing a glimpse of hope."

I pause. I continue.

"Recently, Mom and I were talking about my childhood. She remembered when I was around five years old that I was a sweetheart, but that I was so torn. She retold me a story from one night. She was putting me to bed, and I had asked her 'Mom, did you and Dad give me this skin problem?' And, showing her true form and strong character, she took the blame. 'Yes, son, we did.'"

I pause. I look away from the struggle. I stare at air. I hold in weakness.

"Did you have a response?"

"Yeah, I said, 'That's okay, I still love you.' When she told me that story, I couldn't believe I had asked that, and, most of all, I couldn't believe she took the blame. It makes me very proud, but, at the same time, filled with anger. She took the blame. She blamed herself for my pain."

Holy shit. This better work. *It will, Luke.* I look down at my shoes.

Handman sees beneath my mask. He sees despair.

We sit in silence.

A couple of minutes later, Handman speaks.

"Well, Luke, thanks for sharing today. That took a lot for you to open that one up. This is part of the healing process. Uncovering those repressed memories and searching them for meaning."

"All right, doc, I better go. Take care." I keep the mask on.

"You too, Luke."

I leave.

02/19/08, Session Nine: Coach P

7:00 am

I wake up. Stomach. Knives. Axes. Fists. Gag. Clench. My pants are wet. I look at my hand. I'm holding an empty Sprite can. I passed out with chase in hand. I look around. I'm sitting up on the couch. The TV is on. My intestines rip apart. I grimace. I curse. I walk to the bathroom. I puke. I have to go see Handman. I hate morning. I shower. I look for my mask. I find my mask. I put on my mask.

8:00 am

"So, Luke, I recall earlier in our sessions you mentioning something about a basketball coach who took away your passion for sports. Would you like to get into that?"

"Might as well. That's what I'm here for." My stomach clenches. My facial expression stays consistent.

"Going into grade ten, I was pumped to play high-school ball. I tried out for the senior team, which usually only took one grade-ten student, if any. My buddy Rob and I made it to the final cut. I didn't make the team, but Rob did. And I was fine with that. Rob stood a few inches taller and had a bigger build, so I didn't stress over it. The coach told me to go dominate on the junior team and a spot would be ready for me next year on the senior team. Going to tryouts for the junior team, I was filled with confidence, and ready to help take a team to a championship run. But from the get-go, I didn't get along with the coach. I'll just call him Coach P, not for confidentiality reasons, but because I don't give two shits about him. Anyhow, we didn't like each other. He was one of those coaches who felt insecure

going into coaching, so he picked on some of the players. I wasn't
having any of that, especially from a coach. So when he would say
something to me or another player, I would shoot something right
back. When he called me or another player gay or dumb, I called
him a pathetic clown. This went on the whole season. We wouldn't
even make eye contact in the halls at school. He brought out a bad
side of me. I didn't want to have to say the shit I said, but I also
couldn't let him walk over me and my teammates. I remember this
one time; we were at a basketball tournament and the ref was one
of Coach P's buddies. At one point in the game, a player decided to
bear-hug me, not knowing how to play the game. I retaliated and
threw him against the wall. I got kicked out of the game. Coach
P was furious—and with reason. I had just got kicked out of the
game in front of his friend. But maybe if I had had respect for my
coach I would have controlled myself. Anyhow, after the game, my
coach was on my case in front of the team. He berated me, saying
that I'm so gay and that I loved when that guy hugged me. I stared
at him, laughed, shook my head in disbelief, and walked away. The
players were baffled that he had said that. Since I didn't retaliate, he
continued his rant on the bus trip back to St. Albert about my love
for the guy who had bear-hugged me. Turns out, one of the players
on my team came out of the closet a few years later. My coach called
me and others "gay" as if it were a stigmatized disorder. No wonder
that guy kept his homosexuality a secret. He knew his coach would
have harassed him. If a teacher responds like that, how will his peers?
When I heard my teammate had come out of the closet, and thought
back to grade ten, I felt, and feel, awful for him.

"I ended up not playing most of that year. Coach P took me
from point guard and assigned me to shooting guard. I didn't like
practice anymore. I was showing up more for spite. He played me
one game in the quarter-final, during which I helped lead the team
to victory. Then, he didn't play me for a minute in the semi-final,
and we lost. The next year, I naturally didn't make the senior team,
since I had lost skill instead of gaining some through good coaching.
As well, I had lost that spark, the passion. So I went back to tryouts
for the junior team, thinking I could be smart about this and make

amends. It didn't work. Before even a head nod, he made a smart-assed comment. So I told him I was going to make the team and good luck coaching me. The new guys trying out asked me if I was going to be captain. I laughed, saying it would be a surprise if I made the team. They were confused but later found out what I meant. Rob was still on senior, improving his skill, while I was wasting my time. Coach P put me on the team. I was still starting-line junior-squad calibre. He wouldn't play me. I practically gave up. I wanted to quit but didn't want to give him the satisfaction. Eventually, he ended up cutting me mid-season, because of my poor attitude. He did this after we had gotten our asses kicked and I hadn't moved off the bench for team huddles, because I wasn't being played—again. I could have won that game—again. I said, 'All right, good luck with that.' Throughout that week he tried to get my jersey. I ignored him. Then, one night, he called my house. My Dad, already wanting to wring this guy's neck, answered the phone. We had the Boyd's, our closest family friends, over for dinner. Matt and I were watching TV in the other room, and I silently picked up the phone to eavesdrop. Dad asked him why he acted younger then the kids. Dad told him that basketball was his son's passion and he kicked ass at it. Coach P said he'd call the cops. Dad laughed and told him to go right ahead, before he hung up. Back at school, P kept persisting. He walked into my shop class. A buddy and I had finished our projects, so we were hanging out in the main room. He asked to speak to me. I told him to say what he had come to say. He asked me as nicely as he could, biting his tongue, for the jersey back. I told him the jerseys are for the best players and I was the best he had. He said I was being a little shit. I laughed, shook my head, looked into his eyes, and told him to fuck off. First and last time I swore at a teacher. That day, I got called to the principal's office. I sat down. He told me what Coach P had said. I told him, without going into detail, that he was the worst coach I'd ever had. My principal had seen me play ball in the past, and he agreed I was a good ball player. He told me that while I should be the captain and starting point guard, there wasn't much he could do. I told him Coach P had taken me away from point guard the previous year. I was a shooting guard now. Or had been.

He said it was all word of mouth, and I should be the bigger man, and give the jersey back. I said a big man would get rid of that guy. I said I was happy to be off the team, because I could learn more by teaching myself outside on my driveway and that the only ones left to suffer were the ones he was coaching. He acknowledged this, and I got the figurative slap on the wrist. When I left, I was sure he wasn't going to think twice about my claim. P kept coaching. The players expressed to me that they wished I were on the team and that they hated playing for a joke. Anyhow, I gave the jersey back, after I had a little fun with it. Later on that year, I went to boarding school to play on a team that would have dominated my old team." I let out a deep sigh. That was a lot of talking.

"You went to boarding school? Your life never took an easy route, did it?" he says jokingly.

I enjoy his humour. I laugh.

"No, sir. That would make life too easy. But, yeah, I went halfway through grade eleven, right after I got cut. A family friend, Max, had started going to this boarding school in British Columbia. My parents said it was a prestigious school, and, since my marks were slipping, it would help me raise my grades to get into university. They said they would see if I could try out for the basketball team. After a week of thought, I figured, why not? We went down there over the Christmas holidays to check it out. After some examinations to test my academic skills, and an interview to assess my personality, they said I was eligible to attend the school. A kid had been expelled in Max's dorm, so I took his spot after the holidays. Since it was one of the best high schools in Canada, it wasn't cheap. We didn't have much money. The business was small at this time, so my Dad worked on the side buying, fixing, and selling cars to pay the twenty-five-grand tuition. When I got there, the basketball coaches offered me two tryouts with the team. They only had a senior team, who were really good—the best the school had had in twenty-four years. That first tryout, I was on my game. It was my first time on the court since getting cut, and I had something to prove to myself. I made the team on that one tryout. The coaches said they didn't need to see more. I ended up being the three-point shooter. The starting line was dominant. Amazing flow. Max was the point guard, and I can tip my hat and say he was a better play maker—and it's just weird that a five eleven white boy can dunk. For grade eleven I was the sixth man. Grade twelve ..." *As your drinking progressed.* "... I was the sixth or seventh man. It was good. We had good seasons. We didn't end up on top as we expected, but we had a few tournament wins and breakthrough years for the school. I liked our team. The first year, the guys on the team were all in grade eleven, and we were all pretty good buddies. There were some good times at boarding school."

"Hmm. That is interesting. Well, Luke, again I thank you for opening up. You are showing a desire to get help and are putting yourself back into your past memories, helping you open up those sealed vents. I think we should pick up on your boarding school experiences next time."

"There's not much to know. I learned discipline, I made many good friends from all over the world, and I got into every school I applied to. All in all, it worked out for the best."

"I'm happy to hear that. How about we schedule a time for next week, and we will go from there?"

"Sounds good, Dr. Handman." We schedule a session.

"Take care, Luke."

"Later."

I walk to Jimmy. I think back to boarding school. If only he knew the truth about that experience.

8:00 pm

I drive home from work. I've been telling myself all day I'm not going in there. I pull into the parkade. I say, "Luke, don't be an idiot." I park Jimmy. I walk through the parkade, up the stairs, and through the foyer. I say, "Luke, you're stronger than this. You don't need booze. Wait till the weekend to party with your friends." I walk to the public parkade. I see grey. I have obsessed all day about not going in there. I take the tunnel. I follow my footsteps. I walk through the beer cooler. I say to myself, "If you say you won't, and you do, you're showing a lack of control." I grab the mistress. I take the elevator to my apartment. I sit on the couch. I say, "Fuck it." I swig. Boarding school is on my mind. I decide to look at my graduation year yearbook.

Initially when we talked about boarding school, it was so I could get into the universities I wanted and play basketball. When I agreed, it wasn't those two things that got me to go. I had known since grade ten that I drank for a different reason than others. Hiding to drink alone was becoming depressing and frustrating. I thought boarding school, with their strict policies, would be a perfect way to get away from booze. I figured if I went to boarding school for the rest of high school, I could prove to myself I didn't have to drink, and it wouldn't bother me not having it around. And when I initially went there, that's what happened. I stayed away from booze. I didn't search for a way to drink. I just followed orders to a certain degree. I enjoyed it. I felt good. I still drank a couple of times that year, but only when it was handed to me, or when we would be on a leave weekend and we could go hang out in Vancouver. No extra effort on my part to find booze, just an average teen getting shitfaced with his buddies. But after that summer, going into grade twelve, my mind had changed. I had enjoyed the thrill from getting away with it, and it sure the hell helped pass time.

In grade twelve, Sergio "the Italian stallion", Jay-Young, our North Korean —just kidding—South Korean buddy and I shared a room. We got the coveted bedroom at the end of the hall – furthest from the teachers, that had a separate door that the other residents at the dorm didn't have access to. I needed that room. I wanted that room. I signed up for that room. I sucked up to the teacher to get that room. I initiated conversations about himself and his interests. I cracked small jokes referring to that room. I did this so he would associate that room with me. I got that room. The reason I wanted that room was to keep my private drinking safe and easy. It helped me slip out, and it helped me stay a kept secret.

I'll outline how I was able to drink regularly with our strict allowances. We were given eight bucks a week, which isn't even enough for a mickey. I didn't have personal cash from home, going into grade twelve, because that money had gone to drink already. So I did a few things. I sold my Mom's home-baked cookies. I had told her all my friends loved them, and we hoped she would bake a few dozen. She's very kind, bless her. I sold them. I sold food that I brought from home. My bottom closet would be full. I told my parents I hated the food there, so we would stock up. I wasn't lying. I did hate it. But I ate the cafeteria food, so I could sell the food for booze. I gambled or saved my birthday and Christmas money. Whatever it was, I always found a way. But I never stole from friends or strangers. In truth, I did lie to get money from my parents. When I went on leave for weekends or holidays, I stored booze or asked for money from my folks to go out with the boys. I took that money to buy booze and hide it in my suitcase. That booze could only last so long. I couldn't fill the whole suitcase, just enough not to get busted. Sometimes, we would get someone who lived near the school to get us our booze. You know in the movie *American Pie*, when that guy hands out the boxes of condoms? Everyone gets a box, and then there's the main character, Jim, who is standing anxiously waiting for his half dozen boxes. That's what it was like for me with the alcohol. Except I couldn't do that too often, because I didn't want my friends to think I had a problem. I drank behind their backs. I exposed enough to show I was a partier, but not enough to show I had a serious problem. And I didn't expect my friends to catch on. We were high-school kids, and alcohol is the coolest shit in the world. Sadly, that's how it's viewed.

Here are some close-call stories:

A few of the grad students decided to have a bonfire, just off school property. Over a dozen students came out. Within a couple of hours, it was broken up by police. Some people scattered, and others waved the white flag. I had learned how to deal with this situation, so I let my gut take over. Broken-up bush parties in St. Albert had helped prepare me for this situation. I hid behind a tree. I didn't flee and get chased. I didn't get stage fright and freeze. I crept behind a tree and stood there, motionless, waiting for them to be distracted before I made my move. As a cop caught a couple of runners and took down their names, another headed in the direction where a few of us were hiding. A couple of girls, a little too drunk, were rustling the leaves.

"I hear people over there! Come out right now, or else I will let the dog go!" the lady cop snapped. Her fake dog was obviously not with her.

I could see the cop from the left side of the tree and the girls kneeling behind a bush to my right. They looked hopelessly drunk.

"We're—*hiccup*—not here."

I smiled. Funny line.

The other girl quickly noticed what her friend had said.

"Shit. You busted us!" She was pissed. They got up and took one for the team. This was the crucial part. I knew that I had to get into my bed before the police had a chance to call the headmaster, who would then call the head dorm teachers, who would then search our rooms and take count of who was missing. As the girls got close to the cop, I looked over at two guys, gave them the nod, and bolted. All I heard was a faded, "Heyyy—" from the cops. We were gone. I don't know who those two were. It was pitch-black, and, by the time we saw light, we had separated to our dorms. Getting back into the dorm was the tricky part. I found out later the security guard had noticed a couple of dorms had stubs keeping the doors ajar and, knowing we were off property, had notified the police. He should have called the school first. When I got back to the dorm, in mid-stride I noticed the door was shut. I quickly reached the window to my room, which I had left open—Plan B. But these were tricky windows. They opened at a forty-five degree angle and were only about two feet wide and a foot long. They were designed so students couldn't climb through them. Later, my friends and I stood outside staring at the window wondering how I had gotten through. I took a beating getting in that window, but adrenaline saved my ass. Once I got through, I fell to the floor, quickly got up, jumped into bed, and pretended to be asleep. A minute later, I heard footsteps. The teacher opened the door, turned on the light, and looked around. After he turned the light back off and had gone, I sat up and caught my breath. I turned on my reading light and then noticed my roommates hadn't made it back. They hated me for that one. They were pissed. You could count on one hand the times they did something wrong between the two of them, but you would need a personal Day-timer to schedule around my deeds of defiance. That story, I'm proud of. Most, if not all, stories I tell are of shame, but this one took skill. If I hadn't been such a drinker, I wouldn't have gotten away with it. *Learned behaviour* is what the shrinks call it. Experience taught me how to escape. I don't remember how many of us got away. I never found out if those two guys made it into their dorms. After that night, people starting saying they'd never seen someone do so much shit and not get caught. They hadn't seen much. They told me this while I was walking to my dorm from sport, while they were picking weeds for Wilbur Force. *Wilbur* is when you disobey the rules (and get caught). Wilbur consists of an average of eight days of labour and running: three hours of labour after class and a total of thirty laps around a large pond. Students would still have all the other responsibilities of meal attendance, school, sport, fine art, study sessions, chapel, and homework. Near the end of Wilbur, the students would be in rough shape, especially the not-so-fit students. The extent of trouble the student was in depended on the degree of mischief and the persuasion/lying abilities of the student. I replaced an expelled kid when I arrived. Good thing I didn't follow his footsteps. Only bad kids get in trouble. I'm an angel.

In Alberta the legal drinking age is eighteen. In BC, where my school was, the legal age is nineteen. That wasn't going to stop me from celebrating my eighteenth birthday the right way—the Albertan way. A friend in the dorm made us Yukon IDs. There weren't many people from Yukon living in BC. The liquor-store owners hadn't seen one to compare to. It was a solid ID. For my birthday, we asked the teachers if we could go to Boston Pizza. After we got dropped off, we walked to the nearest liquor store. We stocked up and snuck it into Boston Pizza, making our rye pops cheaper. After getting tipsy at BP, we decided to try our luck with the IDs at the pub. We got in successfully. And we got completely shitfaced. Well, I know I did. I don't remember the night. I was told—as I've often been told by others of my blackout stories—that when we got back, about four of us started wrestling in the foyer. We were a bunch of drunks. A teacher caught us and ordered us to bed. He had to have let that one slip. We drank beer and rye that night. We reeked. I had a blackout. We can classify that one as a lucky warning. A birthday present.

One weekend, near graduation time, we all decided to drink. Even a couple of day students stayed to drink with us. We all hung out in my room, keeping the drinking in the bathroom, since it had the door that locked. As the night progressed, it got a little out of control. All I remember is a couple of guys getting busted—I should have been, too. Knowing we were busted, I crept to my bed, hoping to go unnoticed. Our head teacher, Mr. O, a tall, kind-hearted man, walked into my room while I was hopping into bed. I crawled under my sheets.

"Luke, are you okay? Why are your eyes red?" Mr. O asked, looking for a confession.

"It's my allergies, sir. It's spring; you know me," I said, scratching my eyes, looking for pity.

Mr. O looked at me knowingly. He nodded.

"Get some sleep."

"Thank you, sir. Goodnight."

This isn't adding up. Let's explore behind the scenes. Everything has an underlying cause to it. Alcohol abuse has an underlying cause that triggers the self-inflicted addiction. My free passes must have been a trigger from an underlying cause. I don't know if I'm right about this, but let's see what we can find through my thoughts and perspectives of the scenario.

First, I'll let you in on a secret. If you listen to people carefully and find their likes, dislikes, strengths, and/or weaknesses, you can be anyone you want, depending on the fit of that person. I chose to get on the good side of people—for the most part. I'm talking about people I would have to deal with in times of trouble, such as the teachers, suck-up students, and higher-up students (there are lots of classifications and hierarchy at boarding school). And I did a good job at that. I listened, was polite, gave compliments, agreed to stuff I laughed at in my head, and so on. The mind is the most powerful tool. It's its own identity. If you use it right, a lot of good can happen.

In my case, I have used it for good and bad. I treat myself like shit without burdening others' lives. At boarding school, I did what I could to make having me as a student a breeze for the teacher, if not gratifying. It built respect and trust. It's the foundation of my low profile.

We've already established that I built strong rapports. What else? I had an "in", being placed in my dorm. I had requested and was placed in Dux, because my buddy, Max, was in that dorm. But that was my overt request. In my head, I knew the basketball coaches ran that dorm. And if I were to make the team, I was sure they would give me some leeway, not wanting me to get busted. And it helped having three of the starters in Dux and me as the sixth/seventh man. But the thing is, like I said, I wasn't a starter. Not the best player. My glory days of basketball were grade nine and under. At that point, I wasn't even playing the position I'd grown up playing. I was good, and a contributor to the best team the school had had in decades, but not significant enough.

I'm a quick drinker. I can chug a mickey in seven seconds. It saves time. It quickens the effect. I expect only those who have seen my freak display of chugging to believe it. It's one of the reasons I could drink behind others' backs without suspicion. I could do it fast. At first, drinking that fast messed me up, and I was a noticeable drunk, but, after my tolerance increased, a mickey was the perfect amount to function. It got to the point where, near the end of grade twelve, I would wake up on Sundays and wait for my roommates to go to brunch. I would then chug a mickey in a sip, do shit-all for a few hours, then chug another mickey in the early evening and pass out by 9:00 pm. Best sleep of the week. I got out *just in time*, because the effect was starting to wear off. By graduation, I needed more than a mickey to feel anything, which meant more money, work, and an increase in bust potential. *Just in time* is a common term for a closet drinker. A "successful" closet drinker.

I roomed with two good students with perfect records. We never attracted the attention of the teachers. When things went bad, and a potential bust was in progress, I would slowly creep to my room, where my roommates were usually studying. I would sit at my desk pretending to do the same. The teacher would come in, nod in appreciation of our hard work, and leave. My roommates and I would all start laughing, knowing I had avoided a bust. They couldn't believe I had never been busted. It became a joke. It became a game. I would then go pass out, and they would go back to studying. Even though they got busted once, at that bonfire, it wasn't severe, because neither had been caught for anything before. Serge had been there five years and Jae-young four years.

This still doesn't seem to be enough to explain how I got away with that much drinking. But maybe if we were to add up all the little things it would lead to the shrug of the shoulder. The teacher who pondered, "Ah, Luke's a good kid. I'll let it slip. He's good to have around. He doesn't do this stuff often." Surprisingly, I only got busted for drinking twice. The last one was near the end of the school year, and the other on my birthday, by a different teacher who may not have discussed it with the other staff. I'm not mentioning the other potential busts because of their unoriginality and my cloudy memory. The memories are not ones of accomplishment. I was deeply ashamed of not being able to stay sober. I was never proud, but rather, relieved I could keep it a secret.

I've never revealed the real truths about my boarding school years in full. I tell one friend one story and another friend a different story. I don't reveal enough for anyone to clue in. It goes to show that anyone can have a problem, but if they're intelligent enough to keep their issues to themselves their lives can slowly fade away in isolation.

Intelligent? "Fuck memories." I finish off the bottle. *They'll be gone when you die. That won't be much longer at this pace.* "I'm sick of your shit." *Then stop drinking. It's obvious you have a problem.* "I'm going to fix it on my own, so it's not permanent." *Alcoholism is permanent, Luke.* "Stop saying that fucking word!" I throw the yearbook at the wall. I walk to the bathroom. I brush in darkness. I stumble to my room. I bang my head on the door. I groan. I take off my clothes. I lie in bed. I don't fall asleep. I put on my clothes. I walk downstairs. I buy a bottle. I'm fucked. I sit on the couch. I stare out the balcony windows at the building-lit sky. I chug. I am who I am. I hate who I am. I'm a loser. I'm everything I hate. I finish the bottle. I go to bed. I pass out.

Grace took me to the Comic Strip for my birthday. We had a great time. We sat beside a heckler making comments throughout the sets. I find these types of people to be funny, and so did Grace. We laughed more at the guy than the stand-up comedian. At one point in the night, we looked in each other's eyes while laughing. Her eyes sparkle when she smiles. Her smile brightens my day. At that moment, I felt hope. I felt I could conquer my problem, because now I have her. As a birthday present, she gave me a sweater, sandals, and CD. All of them have meaning. The sweater, because I'm a bum and don't clothes shop. The sandals, because I walk downstairs to greet her in bare feet, and she thinks it's gross. I think it's funny she thinks it's gross. And a CD from the movie *Juno* we liked. I had mentioned I liked a song from the movie. Later in the night, we partied with her friends. She's full of life. A beautiful spirit.

Two weeks ago I realized I had fallen in love. It was Valentine's Day. Grace was sick. She looked gorgeous, as always. I looked into her eyes. My heart grew. I smiled. I knew. She asked what was on my mind. I said she looked beautiful. She smiled and blushed. I didn't tell her I had fallen in love with her. It was Valentine's Day. Too cheesy. I've fallen in love.

03/12/08, Session Ten: Mediator

9:30 am

I wake up to my phone. My parents are driving me nuts. I can't do shit on a hangover. One called after the other. I couldn't listen to them. All they do is bitch about each other. I'm glad I didn't listen. My stomach curdles. I gag. My stomach cuts. I grimace. My stomach splits. I curse. My stomach gets winded. I curse. I ride it out. I shower. I find my mask. I hate this.

11:00 am

I walk into Handman's office. I don't say a word. I sit down.

Dr. Handman sees I'm distraught.

"Are you okay, Luke?"

I cut to it.

"Maybe you were right, Handman. I don't know if I'm up for mediating my parents' relationship. The other night I went to Mom's for two hours to try to reason Dad's side with her. Then I went to Dad's to do the same, and then back to Mom's. It feels like a hopeless cycle. I know they can be friends, because the problem with them right now is resentment and over-analyzing on both their parts. But, in reality, they don't want to hurt each other. They still love each other, but they can't see through the resentment. Especially for Mom, since Dad is dating now. She isn't ready to, because she is still in the grieving process. They each feel the other is out to get them. Which is logical in such a situation, but, fuck, a kid can only hear so much from his parents, especially when I was completely oblivious to all this a couple of months ago."

I pause.

"I don't want to give up on them, but they are giving up on each other. It's making my job of trying to mediate them stressful. I kind of have a lot on my plate right now. I have a new job, an extensive research paper to write, a new girlfriend, and my boxing." *Plus you drink like a depressed fool.* "It doesn't sound like much, but it's enough to affect my daily rhythm. You know what I mean?"

"Of course, Luke. You have your own life, which at the moment isn't what you want it to be. You have to work on yourself before you can help others."

"But if I ignore them to selfishly focus on myself, I can't help them. And I personally believe I'm the only one who can help them. Dave could, but he's gone. And I'm a psych student; it's good practice."

"It's different when you work with family than with clients."

"I understand that, and you know why that is? Because family is much more important than any client is. So, who am I to neglect my own flesh and blood?"

"That's a good point, Luke. But I think your parents would understand if they knew it was having a negative impact on you."

"I never said it was negative. I just feel, like you said, that I haven't found happiness within myself, so it's hard to mediate and hear fresh stories every day when, in my mind, they were the perfect couple throughout my whole life. They are the driving force who pulled me through my struggle. But times have changed. I haven't been home since I was sixteen. They were fine when I left."

"Do you think your leaving had anything to do with it?"

"No—if anything, I thought I was doing everyone a favour. I would never tell them this, but my leaving gave my parents and my brother an opportunity to build their relationships after lost time spent caring for me."

"Well, maybe after you and your brother left the house they became distant. It's a common occurrence."

"I know it's common. I'm sure that's what happened. I'm not trying to unravel how it happened; all I want to do is find a way for them to communicate—without grudges—so they can see the love is still there and always will be there. And I want to hear as little bashing as I can. I know when shit hits the fan, like a divorce, it's hard not to bash. I don't blame them, but they have to realize who they are talking to."

Handman gives me a look of concern. He sees my tension.

"I understand."

I understand what he means by *I understand*.

"I'm going to keep doing what I'm doing; there's really no way to talk me out of it. My girlfriend thought it might be too much for me to handle, too, but you both would do the same. It's just …" I sigh. "… Mom's hurting pretty bad. Dad has moved on, and Mom still suffers. I know things will die down when she becomes ready to date, but she's not there, and Dad is. I don't think she should date right now, anyway, because—she is right—she is still in the early stages. So, my main focus is Mom and trying to keep her grounded and to not let her emotions get the best of her. She just got separated and just had a surgery that didn't go well. So she has had a rough go lately. Not to mention she is an emotional little French lady. That, combined, creates a lot of tears. It's times like this that I wish I were still a kid and the one suffering. But, really, it's just as tough to watch and not feel someone's pain. Makes me realize what she went through."

"You two have a close bond. You love her a lot, don't you?"

"She will always be my number-one gal. She's a tough lady. I've learned a lot from her."

"It sounds like it. Well, Luke, if you feel you can handle the task then I say you do what you have to do."

"Sounds good. Well, I better be off. Take care, Handman."

"See ya, Luke."

7:00 pm

I ignite Jimmy. I leave Gavin's house. He's my "TV talker" autistic client. *TV talker* means he will watch movies, commercials, TV shows, and memorize lines, and repeatedly repeat them. It can be pretty funny. He will do the whole narration with many characters.

He's a great kid with a great heart. Wouldn't hurt a soul. He would be content being on his own with a set of beads. He has an obsession with beads. They provide him with sensory input. They are also a great incentive for him to work hard, because then he gets to play with them. I have been working with Gavin since I started working last summer. My job is to help him prepare himself for the future. He's Connor's age, seven. They are similar, but completely different, like every child with autism. Social interaction is a big factor with autism. Some children with autism have photographic memories, or can equate any math problem, or skillfully play instruments. The list goes on. But when it comes to communication, they don't understand the same way we do. We don't consider slang talk or metaphors as abstract communication. For most children with autism, their thought patterns are concrete. "Completing that puzzle was a piece a cake" would confuse an autistic child; he would compare the puzzle to a piece of cake. "It's raining cats and dogs" would have the child looking out the window for cats and dogs. Gavin makes me laugh a lot. He's very unique and an interesting character. We have a good rapport. He likes that I'm active. He likes when I jump really high on the trampoline and land right beside him. He'll count down from three, and on blast off! I will fall on the tramp, and he laughs hysterically. He could do this for hours. Unfortunately, I can't. My drinking is causing harm to my athletic ability. I'm running out of energy. I get pains when I try. I muscle through it to hide weakness, but it takes away the fun of sport. It's eliminating my motivation for boxing and daily activities. I'm starting to fade. I can't lose these kids. There's so much for us to do. If I lose myself, I lose them. I have lost control on keeping myself. Time will eventually decide my fate.

03/24/08, Session Eleven: Losing Grace

9:00 am

I wake up. Guilt is killing me. Grace is hurting. I'm the cause. She's confused. She doesn't get why I'm getting worse each day. My moods, energy, and mind are fading with time. She's watching me dig my grave, not understanding why. I want to tell her. I need to explain myself. I'm ashamed. I can't tell her. Silence. Stomach. Storm. Pain. Jolt. Thunder. Clench. Gag. Curse. Karma. I'm a prick. I'm losing her. I know how to stop it. I'm not. I want to. I love her. I hate myself. She cries tears of lost hope. I cause those tears. It's foggy. My thoughts are empty. I leave my mask at home. I go see Handman.

11:00 am

"What's on your mind?" Handman sees thought.

"Grace."

"Is Grace your new girlfriend?"

"Yeah, we've been dating for a few months now. It was going pretty good at the start, but it's slowly deteriorating. I know exactly what I'm doing, but I don't know why."

"What is it that you are doing?"

I sigh. I'm a prick. I'm aware.

"You name it. For some reason, I have become obsessively jealous over her ex." *It's because you're a drunk.* "Which is dumb on my part, because she fell out of love with the guy and never saw a future with him, but she sees a future with me. But I still start crazy arguments about him. And it could be something that happened awhile ago, which would really be nothing, and I'll bring it up out of the blue. It's as if I have imagined this worst-case scenario, and I'm working to push her back to him. Like I said, I know exactly what I'm doing, but I don't know why."

"Do you have any sufficient reason to be jealous of her ex?"

"Nope."

"Have you always been jealous with girlfriends?"

"No. When I drink I get jealous, but that's alcohol for you. Growing up, I was in a very trusting family who never showed jealousy. I was never exposed to it, and it's something I've always looked down on. I have always known jealousy breaks up relationships and it's the ultimate sign that you don't trust someone. This is tearing Grace apart, because she hasn't done anything wrong. Yet, I still battle with her, almost trying to persuade her that she is wrong. It's fucked. I know I'm doing it when I do it, and my mind is telling me I'm an idiot while I'm doing it, but I don't stop." I put my head in my hands. Guilt. Shame.

"Can you give me an example?"

I pause to pick one from a haystack of examples. I remove my hands from my face. I look up.

"We were walking in St. Albert the other day, and we saw her ex. He stopped to say hi to Grace. They do the usual hellos. I wasn't listening, because I was looking at the guy wondering if he would be orthodox or southpaw if we were to fight, something that shouldn't enter a normal person's head. It shouldn't be a problem for them to run into each other. People see people. They share the same friends, so there's really no stopping that, and I shouldn't care to stop it. But, somehow, I don't know how to reason using common sense. After the encounter, we walked away, made a little joke about the awkwardness, and went on with our day. I wasn't affected at the time, but …" After a couple of nights of drinking alone and making up scenarios. "… a couple of days later, I accused her of being too happy to see him and shit like that. After that comment, our weekend was ruined, because I didn't let it go and persisted she was thrilled to see him. Does that make any sense to you?" My heart skips a beat. My body tightens. *You're such a shithead.* "I'm such a shithead."

"Don't beat yourself up over it, Luke. You're going through a rough time in your life. It's not easy to make someone happy when you aren't happy with yourself."

"Yeah, I've heard that one before. Recently she told me I enjoy being miserable. That was one of the first times I didn't have a smart-ass response. I just agreed. She also feels she has to censor herself around me, which is something I don't blame her for, because I have over-analyzed every detail to its worst-case scenario. I was never like this." *You were better before the alcohol, Luke.*

"Maybe you shouldn't be in a relationship during this time in your life."

"You kidding me? This girl is the best thing that has happened to me. It's about time I catch a break and get a piece of perfection. We've fallen in love. First time I have said that to a girl. I took her to Jasper Park Lodge for the weekend, a birthday gift from my Mom, and we had a great time together. Near the end of the trip we went for a walk by the lake. As the sun was setting, I told her I had fallen in love with her. She looked into my eyes and said it back. It was a great trip. We played cards, went for walks, went swimming and hot tubbing, had romantic dinners, watched movies, and hit up the mountains." I pause. Why can't I be that guy again? *Because you're slipping. Alcohol is creating this.* It has to be something else.

I notice my silence. I continue.

"It ended well. But, since we have been back, I'm seeing myself slip. I'm becoming paranoid, self-conscious, insecure, and jealous. It's not me. Not how I was brought up. Not who I am. The guy she met in the first few months was for the most part the real me." When I had a stronger mask. "I don't know, Dr. Handman. I really am just lost for words. I don't know anymore. It's useless. I know exactly what I'm doing—to a T. If I can identify it but not fix it, what's the use?" I sink into the leather. Life is losing colour. Lights are fading into shade. What is going on? *You're losing it.*

"Luke, you need to bring that strength I have seen in you since we began our sessions. You have to realize your life has been tough, and you have overcome a lot and are still in the midst of working on things. But you can't give up. You're better than that. You know that."

I sit passively.

"Yeah, I know that," I mumble.

"Buy your girlfriend some flowers and apologize. Explain to her your situation with life right now. If she loves you, she will understand."

"There's only so much understanding a girl can do without knowing the whole truth." *Nice slip.* "But about the flower bit, I've done that to the point of meaninglessness. I've spent a shitload on flowers. I keep promising to change, and saying I know what's wrong with me, and that I'm working on it, and she has to bear with me, and it will all be worth it. I even admitted that I'm seeing a shrink. But she doesn't understand why, because I can't go into detail. Some things are better left unsaid. She keeps giving me chances, and I love her for that, but I can't do this to her forever. I have caused too much pain and tears. Unwanted, unnecessary tears and pain. I was content when the only life I was ruining was my own. I want to let her go, so she can be happy. At the same time, I want her, knowing I can make her happy, but I just need to fix some kinks. But I wouldn't put up with me for another day. I don't know how she does it."

"Well, it sounds like you two are going through a rough patch, but that's what happens in relationships. This is your first love, Luke. It's not going to be perfect."

"Our relationship couldn't be further from perfect right now. And it's only been a few months. All I can give her is material goods. And that's meaningless. You can only buy love for so long, and, when you deal with a girl that doesn't care about material goods, it's even tougher. I just need to fix my shit soon, Handman. I'm serious. We have to do this man. I lose her, I'm done."

"Yes, Luke, we have to get to the core of the problem. It's just after noon, though. We'll have to pick up from here next session. What do you think?"

I sit passively. I stare at my shoes. I don't hear a word. Grace is on my mind. *She's the best and sweetest thing that has happened to you. Only a drunk would ruin that for the bottle. You're becoming a waste of my time.* "Good. Get out of here." *Get rid of the booze and I'm gone.*

"What? Oh yeah, sure." I catch the last bit he says after a delay and recall. I get up and leave. I forget to say bye.

04/08/08, Session Twelve: The Secret is Revealed

6:00 am

I'm drinking into oblivion. I haven't increased my intake, yet I have been getting really drunk quickly. Every night is a blackout. My intestines are shot. I feel like shit. Yet I buy a bottle. I put it on the coffee table. Unscrew the lid. Dry heave. Chug. Feel my stomach curdle. Run to the bathroom. Puke. Go back downstairs. Buy a bottle. Repeat. Then blank. Now I stare at a wall. I'm lying on the floor. I'm in my hallway. My stomach goes through the usual routine of hatred. I ride it out. I hate my life. I need help. I want help.

9:00 am

"Hey, Luke." Handman greets me in the hallway.

"Hey." I'm grabbing a tea.

"Whenever you're ready, I'll be in my office."

"Kay." I put some sugar in my tea and drag my feet to his office. I might have to cancel work today. I haven't had to call in because of a hangover before. Shit. I get to his office. I sit.

He asks how I'm doing.

I stare out the window. I turn to him. I look into his eyes.

"Handman, I have a confession." I pause to read his expression.

He sits up in his chair. He's interested.

I let out a deep sigh. I look at my shoes.

"I have a drinking problem."

He pauses. He sits back in his chair. He's shocked.

"Are you sure, Luke?"

"There's no way around it. I've tried every excuse, every self-help method. I thought I could quit drinking alone when my uncle died. I didn't last a day. I told myself when I told Grace I'm in love with her I'd quit drinking alone. I didn't last a day. I got sleeping pills. I didn't drink for three days because the pills worked initially. After dealing with withdrawal symptoms and the easy sleeps died out, I threw away the pills and bought a bottle. Every day my mind tells me not to drink, but somehow I end up in the liquor store. My first and all thoughts of the day are surrounded by alcohol." I pause and let him digest this.

He sits there absorbing the information.

"Handman, I have been hung over every session we have had so far. And you didn't know. And that's because I have learned to master deception. But I pay you to help me, and I haven't told the truth, because I didn't want to think I had a problem. I thought I could fix it on my own. I wear what I call *masks* to hide my true self. I'm content with hurting myself, but now I'm hurting someone special to me."

"So that's the missing piece to your story."

"Yes. I've wanted to tell you for months. I've wanted to tell anyone, for that matter. The messed-up thing, Handman, is that nobody knows. Nobody has even the slightest idea that I drink alone, every night. I have a girlfriend who doesn't know. I've wanted to tell Grace for a couple of months. It would explain everything. She knows I'm a roller-coaster ride of ups and downs and that, for some reason, I have all the patience in the world for the kids I teach but none for her. That I can be the happiest guy, and, within a second, I'm bitter."

Handman's confused.

"Nobody knows?"

"You didn't. And I see you first thing in the morning. It's about wearing that mask. I can hide my pain well. I can be anyone I want once I get an understanding of the person I'm with. But if anyone is going to bust me for drinking, it's Grace. She's the only one I can't completely hide myself from. I don't really know how I've managed to cover it this long even. I almost want her to bust me. But I'm too ashamed."

Now he's curious.

"How have you been able to get around?"

I expect curiosity.

"Lots of ways. If she's staying over, and I don't have a legit enough excuse for us to drink that night, I wait till she falls asleep. She falls asleep around ten or eleven. Perfect for an insomniac drunk. If we are drinking that night together, we usually split a bottle of wine. Sometimes two. It's plenty for her to get tipsy, but not enough for me to feel a buzz. So, even then, I wait till she's asleep, and finish off whatever wine is left. I then go into my spot, where a bottle will be waiting for me, which I previously bought knowing she was probably going to stay over. If she's over for the evening, but not staying the night, I don't worry about it. I wait till I drop her off. If I have to, I cut it short, so I can go to my liquor store which stays open till midnight. I'm always the driver when we get together, to be nice, but, subconsciously, I know it's so I can control the tempo. She has asked me what happened to the leftover wine from the night before. I would reply that I lost the cork, so it was going to sour, and I dumped it down the drain; that we had finished it, making her feel like a drunk even though she isn't; or that I wouldn't be drinking it anytime soon, since the weekend was over, so I tossed it. If we aren't together that night we usually talk on the phone for a bit before she sleeps. I'll have a couple of swigs while we talk, stay sober till we hang up, and then go to the bottle. Lately, I've been giving her excuses to not hang out if I want to drink alone. And it's progressively getting worse."

"And she has never hinted toward you having a drinking problem?"

"No. She knows I'm miserable, but doesn't know why. She knows of my masks, though. She sees how I act in public and private. I can be the nicest guy to a complete stranger and a cold-hearted prick to her. It's somewhat twisted, but I have said things to make her feel as if she has the problem and not me. I tell her she isn't a conscious drunk and that she flirts too much and dumb shit like that. None of it is true. Half the nights I don't remember, and I ask her questions, only to get some info and turn it around to make her feel guilty. I don't know how I manage to transfer my shit to her, but she either buys it, which makes her feel self-conscious, or she doesn't want to bother fighting with me anymore. She has given up defending herself around me. I'm a horrible person." I sit back in my chair. I look at the ceiling. *It's about time you said something. Now do you hear how messed up you are, Luke? How can you think you're an honest guy, when you have been living a lie?* "I've been living a lie. What do I do, Handman? I'm desperate."

"Have you considered AA?"

I close my eyes and shake my head.

"No. I was hoping you wouldn't say that," I mumble.

"Well, Luke, when it comes to alcoholism, there is no cure. And AA is well known for being a great support group for alcoholics. A lot of success stories come from there."

"Whoa, whoa! What's this *alcoholic* talk? This is temporary." I tense up. Paranoia strikes. *He's trying to help you Luke.* Screw this. "All right … whatever … I'll check it out. But I'm telling you this hoping we can work out my shit so I don't have to quit drinking for life."

"We will discuss it further next session. Let's not wait too long, though. We should get into this soon. Can you come by in the next couple of days? Preferably early?"

"Yeah, I can try. As an insomniac drunk, I hate early mornings. But, sure."

"Okay, Luke, come in a couple of days—on Thursday, at 8:00 am. Try not to drink till then. If you feel like drinking, give me a call."

"Sounds good," I say, and then I leave.

I walk to Jimmy. I cancel work. I drive home. I puke. I shower. I sleep.

8:00 pm

I sit on the couch, bottle in hand. I can't get AA out of my thoughts. Only old people go to AA. I'm too young. I pick up my laptop. I turn on the computer. I go to Google. I don't want to type it in at the top. Someone might notice the site if they use my computer. I type in Alcoholics Anonymous. I click on an option. The home page pops up. Near the bottom there is a section called "Is AA for you?" I click on it. It asks to fill out a questionnaire.

1—Have you ever decided to stop drinking for a week or so but only lasted for a couple of days?

Most of us in AA made all kinds of promises to ourselves and to our families. We could not keep them. Then we came to AA. AA said: "Just try not to drink today." (If you do not drink today, you cannot get drunk today.)

Yes–But only made promises to myself. That's half a check.

2—Do you wish people would mind their own business about your drinking—stop telling you what to do?

In AA we do not tell anyone to do anything. We just talk about our own drinking, the trouble we got into, and how we stopped. We will be glad to help you, if you want us to.

No–No one knows.

3—Have you ever switched from one kind of drink to another in the hope that this would keep you from getting drunk?

We tried all kinds of ways. We made our drinks weak. Or just drank beer. Or we did not drink cocktails. Or only drank on weekends. You name it, we tried it. But if we drank anything with alcohol in it, we usually got drunk eventually.

No–I drink to get drunk. Simple as that.

4—Have you had to have an eye-opener upon awakening during the past year?

Do you need a drink to get started, or to stop shaking? This is a pretty sure sign that you are not drinking "socially."

> **No**–I drink at night after all my stuff is done. My shakes are minor.

5—Do you envy people who can drink without getting into trouble?

At one time or another, most of us have wondered why we were not like most people, who really can take it or leave it.

> **No**–I don't get into trouble.

6—Have you had problems connected with drinking during the past year?

Be honest! Doctors say that if you have a problem with alcohol and keep on drinking, it will get worse—never better. Eventually, you will die or end up in an institution for the rest of your life. The only hope is to stop drinking.

> **Yes**–Paranoia is ruining my life. My intestines are shot.

7—Has your drinking caused trouble at home?

Before we came into AA, most of us said that it was the people or problems at home that made us drink. We could not see that our drinking just made everything worse. It never solved problems anywhere or anytime.

> **No**–I live alone.

8—Do you ever try to get "extra" drinks at a party, because you do not get enough?

Most of us used to have a "few" before we started out if we thought it was going to be that kind of party. And if drinks were not served fast enough, we would go someplace else to get more.

   Yes–But I never noticed anyone stopping at some point in the night when partying. I sneak drinks because I have a higher tolerance than most. I'm just keeping pace.

9—Do you tell yourself you can stop drinking any time you want to, even though you keep getting drunk when you don't mean to?

Many of us kidded ourselves into thinking that we drank because we wanted to. After we came into AA, we found out that once we started to drink, we couldn't stop.

                    Yes–Got me there. I've never had one drink.

10—Have you missed days of work or school because of drinking?

Many of us admit now that we "called in sick" lots of times, when the truth was that we were hungover or on a drunk.

   Yes–But only missed classes I didn't need to attend. Today was the first day of work I missed because of a hangover.

11—Do you have blackouts?

A blackout is when we have been drinking hours or days which we cannot remember. When we came to AA, we found out that this is a pretty sure sign of alcoholic drinking.

   Yes–Most do. Maybe I just get a little more than others.

12—Have you ever felt that your life would be better if you did not drink?

Many of us started to drink because drinking made life seem better, at least for a while. By the time we got into AA, we felt trapped. We were drinking to live and living to drink. We were sick and tired of being sick and tired.

No–I don't see a life without alcohol.

I'm good. I'm not going to check my score. I passed. I take a swig. This is temporary, no big deal. I spilled the secret. It's out. I'm good now. I can drink tonight. I'm getting help. I'll fix it.

6:00 am

Silence. Storm. Axes. Knives. Intestines. Bathroom. Puke. Bed. Defeat. Pain. I stare at the ceiling. Mindless time passes. I'm sick of this. I won't wear my mask today. I don't feel comfortable. I want my mask. I stare at it. I pick it up. I put it down. I leave.

8:00 am

Dr. Handman greets me in the waiting room. He looks at me differently. There is a sense of sorrow in his expression. Now he knows. Is this the way I'll be portrayed if I admit alcoholism – as a sick person? I don't know about this.

"Hey, Dr. Handman." We shake hands.

"Hey, Luke." We walk to his office. We sit.

Dr. Handman starts.

"So, Luke. You took a big step last session. I'm glad you're ready to face your drinking. How long have you known you have a problem?"

"Since I was about sixteen I knew I drank for a different reason than others. I didn't drink to socialize. I drank to heal the pain." I pause. I don't feel like getting into details. The truth is embarrassing, painful, shameful, pathetic.

Dr. Handman takes in the info. He decides how to approach it. He senses I don't want to get into details.

"How about we start away from your consumption and into past history? Is there any one in your family that has or is dealing with alcoholism?"

"Well, there's my uncle who died last year from cirrhosis of the liver at age forty-six. He died in secrecy. He wasn't given a second chance. Then there are a few relatives and my Grandma who passed a couple decades ago. Most recently, my mom has admitted to alcoholism. That one was a shocker for me. Growing up, I never saw an issue. But I guess she drank in secrecy for the last few years. When she told me about it, I was doubtful. I thought if my mom had a problem, how big of a problem do I have? So I wouldn't let myself believe it. When she told me, I asked her how. She told me how she went about, and ended by saying she is a lot happier now that alcohol is out of her life. I told her I was proud of her. I didn't know what else to say. One day I remember being at mom's. We were sitting on the sofa in the living room. On the coffee table, there was a book called *Alcoholics Anonymous*. I picked it up and asked mom if this book has helped her. She said the stories are hard to take, but very inspiring. I asked if I could look at it because I was doing a paper on alcoholism. Mom said of course, because she had another one. I took it home but never looked at it initially. That night, drunk, I picked it up and started reading it. I passed out and woke up later with a book on alcoholism to my left and a empty bottle of vodka to my right. That stab of irony was a dagger to the soul. I knew I was screwed."

"That is interesting. Your family are a rare few who managed to hide their alcoholism."

"I think we'd be surprised to hear how many people can go unidentified. For the quote unquote successful closet alcoholic, no one knows until they admit it. I'm sure if I were to tell people about it right now they would think I'm full of it. That maybe studying psychology has made me paranoid. No one thinks I have a problem, Dr. Handman. And I don't expect anyone to believe me. I've lived a lie, why should anyone believe me?"

"They'll believe you because you'll be telling them the truth."

"But I don't want to have to be an alcoholic. I want to fix this with you, so I don't have to admit anything. I want to take care of it, so it can be forgotten, and no one will ever have to know."

"Well Luke, if you're an alcoholic, then you already have an addiction. The only way out is to be honest. Did you go on that website?"

I put on a mask.

"No I haven't had time. But I haven't had a drink since our last session." I shadow a lie with another lie. I don't want to talk about this anymore. "I'll make sure to do that for next session."

"Okay good. Go on that site when you get home tonight and try not to drink. I think that's great you haven't had a drink yet. Keep it up. You're on the right track."

"Thanks doc." We schedule a time. We shake hands. I leave.

I go to work. I go home, park Jimmy. I take my tunnel of hatred. I drink. I pass out.

04/15/08, Session Fourteen: I'm "Cured"

10:00 am

"Coo, coo."
    "Coo, coo."
    "Coo, coo."
    I wake up. I'm weak. My intestines hate me. I hate my intestines. Every day it's the same routine. Calm. Storm. Knives. Axes. Fists. Gag. Clench. Curse. Life has lost meaning. All colours are now grey; all objects are now hollow. I wonder how long I can last. Uncle Gary tells me I'm not built for it. He's saving me a seat. I say thanks. I need help. I have to find my mask. I see Handman today. I'm sick of lying. I have to. I can't quit drinking. I can't get help. I look for my mask.

10:30 am

I find my mask.

11:00 am

I walk into the waiting room.
    "Good morning. How are you?" I greet the receptionist.
    "Good. Thanks. Take a seat, Luke. Dr. Handman will be with you shortly."
    "Thank you." I take a seat.
    Handman walks in.
    "Hey, doc." I greet him and shake his hand.
    "Hey, Luke."

We walk to his office. We sit.

"So, Luke, how have you been handling sobriety? Have you felt like drinking?"

"No, I'm good. I still haven't had a sip since that session. I went on the AA site. There are a bunch of questions that ask specifics about your life to see if you're an alcoholic. I passed. I don't have a problem. I have just been medicating my depression with a depressant. It's time I get off the hooch. I mean drinking alone. I'll still go out every so often for special occasions, but that's about it. I'm pumped about this, Handman. As if I have had an epiphany. I see what I have to do now. Hopefully this will save my relationship with Grace."

"You do look better today," he says, persuaded by my lie.

"Thanks. I feel better," I say, persuaded by my lie.

"Okay, good. So, let's dig into this then and see why you started to drink. You said you knew you drank for other reasons then socializing at the age of sixteen. When did you notice the addiction starting?"

"Last summer. I was having trouble sleeping. My place was a sauna, and my skin was driving me nuts, so I started having a couple of glasses of wine at night to make it easier. Then it turned into a bottle. But I haven't gone further than a bottle of wine a night." The truth is too ugly. Lies are easy.

"You drank a whole bottle of wine by yourself?" He says this as if it's incomprehensible.

"Yeah, I figured, since they say a glass of wine is healthy, I would quadruple it," I say jokingly.

He stares blindly. I don't think he gets drunk's humour. He probably hasn't finished a full bottle of wine in half a year. How can someone who doesn't drink relate to my stories? What can he do for me? He's a smart, educated guy, but that's the problem. He's not a messed-up, depressed heavy drinker. He doesn't know what I experience. He only knows what the books tell him. Screw this.

"So, anyway, I think I have this figured out. We have traced my tracks, and I thank you for that. I understand I have had a tough go in my past, and I know I repressed my memories, and I think exploring into my past has shed some light on the subject. I'm ready to fix my problem. No matter what, I won't drink alone, and I'll just work out my everyday issues with the power of my mind."

I pause. I show a mask of success and achievement.

"Thank you, Dr. Handman." I shake his hand with passion and persuasion. "Thank you for encouraging me to dig out my repressed memories. You're a good doctor."

Handman wasn't expecting this.

"Are you sure, Luke? There are still areas we can cover. You just quit drinking recently. What if you feel like slipping and drinking alone?"

"Then I'll call you," I smile.

Handman pauses. He's in a shrink block. He pauses. He hesitates. He expresses doubt and confusion. He hesitates. He knows his options. He can't force therapy. I need to want it. He knows. He's smart. He knows I won't quit drinking. I know I won't quit. He knows there's nothing he can do. Who would want to be a shrink?

"Luke, I have to say I have thoroughly enjoyed our sessions. I think we are cutting it a little short, but if you say you are ready, then you are ready. Your life is inspirational, and if you put yourself as your number-one priority, you will succeed beyond limits. You will help all those people you have set out to help since you were a child. Good luck, Luke. I couldn't forget you if I tried."

"Ha ha, good one. Thanks again. I'll always remember you, and I wish you the best with your future endeavours. Take care."

We give the signature man hug, quick pat on the back.

"Never hesitate to call."

"I'll remember that."

"Bye, Luke."

I smile and nod. I walk out of his office for the last time. *So that's it, Luke? You're giving up again?* "Handman doesn't drink. He's great when it comes to his practice, but he doesn't know what heavy drinking is like. He thought drinking a bottle of wine a night was a lot." *Stop calling yourself a heavy drinker. You're an alcoholic, Luke. Time to face the truth. Did you read those questions carefully on the AA site? You beat around the bush on every question. You're headed in the yes column for all of them.* "I'm not there yet. I'll ride it out. I tried. As smart as he is, he can't help me—and screw AA." *You're dying.* "I'm young."

What Happened

05/25/08, St. Albert Rainmaker Rodeo
Weekend: Sunday Morning

I wake up. Grace isn't beside me. I get up. I walk to the TV room. Grace is sleeping on the couch.

"Grace."

She opens her eyes.

"What are you doing?" I ask curiously.

She looks at me.

"Let me guess, you don't remember last night?" Grace is pissed.

"Refresh my memory."

"Luke!" She sits up. "You lost it on me last night! I said hi to Steve, and—" I cut her off.

"What are you doing saying that piece of shit's name?"

"Oh my God! You're unbelievable! I can't do this."

"Can't do what? You can't stand having him out of your life? I remember now. You saw that loser and went up to him to say hi." I tense up. Paranoia sets in. "You're all touchy-feely: 'Oh hey, Steve,'" I say mockingly. I'm making this up. I don't remember the night.

Grace looks baffled.

"I don't get you, Luke. I'm with you. What's your problem?"

"My problem is that you still like the guy." I hear it. I don't get it.

"How many times do I have to tell you this, Luke? I broke up with him because I fell out of love with him. I never saw a future with him. I see a future with you." She pauses and mumbles to herself. "Or so I thought."

"What was that?" I heard her.

"Nothing."

119

"Whatever, Grace. I'm sick of seeing that lanky piece of shit everywhere we go."

"Luke, he is friends with my friends. What do you want me to do? Abandon my best friends in case he is around?"

"Don't make me sound like an idiot."

"You do that on your own." She's witty.

"Funny. I hope you enjoyed sleeping on the leather on a nice summer's day."

"Better than sleeping with you." She's on a roll.

I nod. I appreciate the fight in her. Paranoia sets back in.

"I'm sick of this, Grace. That guy is lucky I don't make him eat shit."

She laughs mockingly. "Why would you beat someone up? That'll only lose me."

"I already lost you."

She shakes her head.

I walk to the bedroom. I shake my head.

"Can you drive me home?"

"I'm going to sleep." I go to sleep.

A couple of hours later, I wake up. Grace is beside me. I hold her. We make up. I drive her home. On the way to her house, paranoia takes me back to last night.

"I can't believe you went up to him." Holy shit. Seriously? *You're insane.*

Grace sits back in the passenger seat. She heaves a big sigh. She's in awe.

"Luke! You can't get mad at me, say sorry, have sex with me, and then get mad at me again. You're using me. You keep fucking doing that!" Grace only swears when she's furious.

"I don't lie to have sex with you. At the time I'm fine. But then logic kicks in, and I realize your motives." Replace *logic* with paranoia. And *realize your motives* with listen to my delusions.

I continue to rant about hating the guy. I don't know him. I'm sure he's a good person. But that's when it's me talking, not this lunatic tearing Grace apart. The words come out. I don't put them there.

"Just take me home." Grace hides her tears. She buries her pain.

The rest of the ride, we sit in silence.

1:30 am

Grace and I are going to Banff in the afternoon. She's sleeping right now. I just puked all over the bathroom. We went to an Edmonton Cracker Cats baseball game tonight. It was for her work at the bank. I had bitched earlier that I was sick of the plans changing. Initially, we were supposed to go to a bar on Whyte Avenue, which would have saved me money on cabs. I got bitter. I've been a prick about it for the last couple of days. Grace had nothing to do with it. Then we went to River Cree casino with the younger crowd from the bank she works at. I drank a couple of beers throughout the night to keep me from doing what I just did. After we were dropped off, I said we should open a bottle of wine. She said that we had all weekend to drink. I said I was going to have a glass, and I poured it. We watched TV. Grace fell asleep on my lap. I carried her to my bed and went back to the couch. I drank the glass of wine, put down the empty glass, and picked up the bottle. In one sip, I chugged the bottle. That wasn't a good idea. It was a nine-dollar bottle and tasted like shit. I immediately felt my gag reflexes. I rushed to the toilet but was too late. I puked all over the bathroom. Luckily it's summer. The fan was on in my room, and the door was shut, drowning out the noise. I quickly cleaned it up. I sprayed air freshener. I hopped in the shower and then went to bed.

We have a long drive coming up.

10:30 am

"Luke."

I wake up. I sit up, dazed. I lie back down.

"Luke."

I open my eyes.

"What?" I hate morning.

"Get up."

"Yeah, yeah."

"Are you having breakfast?"

"No."

"Okay. I'm going to make a bagel, shower, and get ready."

"Good stuff." Calm. Anticipate. Storm. Clench. Knives. Intestines. Axe. Clench. I silently grimace. I stare at the ceiling. I ride it out. The pains subside. I breathe. I hear Grace in the kitchen putting a bagel in the toaster. I get up. I walk to the kitchen. I kiss her on the cheek.

"Morning, beautiful."

"Morning."

Grace looks at the empty wine bottle on the counter. I didn't hide it. If I did, and she found it, or noticed it was missing, it would show I was hiding something.

She looks puzzled.

"Did you drink that whole bottle last night?"

"No. I had a glass. While I was getting packed for today, I put that bottle in the cooler, but figured it was just going to spill all over our food. So I tossed it."

"Why didn't you save it?"

"By the time we get back from Banff and drink it, it'll taste like vinegar. Unless you want me to drink alone on a Monday." I laugh.

"Good point." She kisses me. "Get ready, handsome man."

"Will do."

Grace walks to the bathroom to shower. I walk to my room to prepare for the second wave of pains. I anticipate the thundering jolt. I silently grimace. I ride it out.

I go up to Grace after she has showered and is getting ready. I kiss her. I gesture toward the bed. She tells me she's getting ready. I take it as an insult and give her the cold shoulder. Paranoia is fucking with me. It's not me, but paranoia tells me it is because of me. *Because you're an alcoholic. It's a symptom.* "When are you going to drop it? I'm not an alcoholic." *I'll drop it when you understand.* I feel stupid for acting like a selfish baby. I don't know who this is. This guy is a pansy. I already put doubt in her eyes. We haven't even left for the trip. She's hurting. I'm the cause of her pain. I don't know what to do. I don't know about this trip.

06/30/08, *The Aftermath*

Poor girl. She has had high hopes for us from the start. We've been comfortable talking about moving in together and marriage. Something we both weren't able to talk about in the past. Not till we finish school and start our careers, but, still, it's a topic of consideration. When we talk about it, I can't help but wonder how I could secretly drink while living with someone. It wouldn't be possible. I'd get busted. I talk about it being amazing. I wouldn't want to spend my life with anyone else. I can't live with myself. I'm a train wreck. No more self-loathing. I'm not the victim. Grace is. I'm sitting on my couch. I have a bottle of vodka in hand. I have no plans for the rest of the day. I swig. I reflect on the trip. I've ruined our sex life. It's messed, the way I make up these scenarios in my head. It's embarrassing to talk about. I have turned into a pathetic loser: no confidence, no self-esteem, insecure, jealous, and passive aggressive. We hadn't seen much of each other the past month, since she's working two jobs, and I have my research paper due date coming up. So, naturally, I figure that once we finally get a chance to see each other, she will jump into my arms, wanting sex. But when she sees me and wants to cuddle and watch TV, I get offended. Immediately after that, I realize why I'm offended and feel like an idiot. Paranoia has created this the past few months. It continues on the trip. At one point, I made some smart-ass comment referring to sex. She lost it. I had pushed the limit. She told me I make her feel like a prude, even though we already have lots of sex. I'm creating so much insecurity in this relationship, I'm dumbfounded that we're still dating. This is not how sex is supposed to happen. A strong relationship built on trust, love, and happiness first has to be established, and an amazing sex life will follow. Our sex life was perfect at the start, but I'm slowly slipping and slowly losing her. It's funny, because I know exactly what I'm doing even while I'm battling with her, and yet I don't stop.

Not funny. Sad. Pathetic. Seeing and knowing what I'm doing and not being able to control it—rather than being oblivious—is brutal. Painful. Frustrating.

With the issues I've created, insecurity, resentment, and arguing follows. We've had our fair share of fights the last few days. I've never sworn at Grace. I swear—that's obvious—but not at her. Unfortunately, that ended last night. After a weekend of a few good times and lots of tension and arguing, last night was the last straw for Grace. This is what happened. I was slowly building some trust back. We were cuddling and talking. Grace had her head on my chest, while I sat up and massaged her back. We had just finished watching *Silence of the Lambs*. We're big fans of that series. We were talking about the movie. While we were talking, Grace fell asleep in my arms. Instead of feeling good that my girlfriend felt secure and comfortable falling asleep in my caress, I flipped a switch. I woke her up and bitched that she doesn't give a shit about what I have to say. She couldn't believe I woke her up for that. I couldn't either, after I said it, but once I'd said it, I couldn't go back. She fired back. I brought up past shit. It's what I do when in doubt. I said stuff about her ex. She started crying. She threw a book I was reading called *What Happy People Know,* by Dan Baker, PhD. Another self-healing attempt. But in short order I got the book thrown at me. I said, "Fuck you," in a nonchalant tone. I was sitting on the bed and picking up the book with my leg. Grace was standing at the end of the bed. She said, "Pardon?" in a tone that gave me an opportunity to take back what I had said. Instead of taking that opportunity, I again mumbled, "Fuck you," while I stared at the blank TV.

Grace ran into the bathroom, crying. I took this opportunity to chug some leftover drinks. Her leftover drinks. I don't have leftovers. It was quiet in the bathroom. I went to the door and asked if she was okay. She told me to leave her alone. I told her it wasn't safe to be in the bathroom with a locked door in case she passed out. She wasn't drunk. She told me she was fine. I told her I was going to knock the door down. I pushed the door. She opened it. I told her to dump me—egging her on. She said no. I said it again. She said no again. I told her I knew she wanted to, so she should do it. She said, "Fine," shoved me from the doorway, and walked toward the bed. I said she was probably happy. Now, she could be with her piece-of-shit ex. She couldn't believe I had said that. I couldn't believe I had said that. She had a meltdown. I'd never seen her melt down. I don't think she had, either. I realized I had just caused a happy girl to break down. I tried to soften the blow. I gave her a pity speech. I said drunken shit: "I'm just lost. I'm fixing it. I love you. I don't know why I'm doing this. I don't know why I can't make the girl I love happy. I want to make you the happiest girl. You deserve happiness." I've said this speech a dozen times. I finished by saying, "I'm fixing it." She forgave me. She said she didn't want to break up. Baffled, I said I didn't want to either. She went back to bed. I massaged her back. She fell asleep. I left the room. I walked outside. I walked to a pub. I sat down at the bar beside a couple of old men. I ordered a triple vodka and watched UFC fights. I ordered three more triples. I went back to the room, showered, and brushed my teeth. I went to bed. I grabbed Grace in my arms. I passed out.

I keep my secret hidden. I leave Grace with no answers or clues to my behaviours. I've become accustomed to my lie of a life. I've become accustomed to misery. It's a part of me now. I take a swig. I'll never learn. Alcohol has become my number-one priority. It has become my curse. The bottle is my ammo of self-destruction. I'm letting alcohol win. I hate losing. I'll always end up on my couch, bottle in hand. Alcohol is taking over my life. Alcohol is my life. I can't live with alcohol. I can't live without alcohol. I found my girl. I will lose her to my mistress. I'm going to miss her. I miss myself. I used to think I was pretty cool and charming. Now I'm everything I hate. *Because you're a typical alcoholic.* "Get over it, will you. I'm not quitting." *I'm not quitting.*

Holy shit. This has to be it. Grace can't live like this. I can't live like this. I'm sitting on the couch. I'm drinking. Last night was our official six months together. We planned to celebrate it today. I forgot. I thought it was today. I reflect on last night and today.

I'm home from buying Grace a pearl bracelet to match her necklace, along with some flowers. I place her gift on the table. I grab my bottle of vodka. I go to the couch. I start to chug. Mid-chug, I hear someone banging on my door. I hide the booze. I look through the peephole. It's black. I try to open the door. It doesn't open. Paranoia tells me I'm locked in. Someone is out for me. I'm slipping. I frantically try to open it. I can't. I look through the peephole again. It's black. I don't know what's going on. I make up scenarios. I'm going to be kidnapped. There are terrorists about to bomb my door. I start pacing. My heart pounds. I pace. I go back to the door. I realize I've locked the door. I unlock the door. I open it. It's Grace. She asks what took so long. I tell her the story, excluding my delusions. I ask her why she covered the peephole. She says she was kidding around and laughs. I laugh. I'm relieved she isn't a kidnapper or terrorist. I realize I must smell from the booze. She notices her gift. I grab a piece of gum. I ask why she's over. She says she dropped someone off from work in my neighbourhood and thought she would come see me on our anniversary. I ask if it's tomorrow. She says I'm a goof and that tomorrow is the day we're celebrating, because she was supposed to work late tonight. I reassure her I knew that. I am still a little confused from the lock-in (mind) game I played on myself. She asks what I'm doing. I say I was just getting ready to go watch the fights with the guys in St. Albert. I don't tell her I planned to drink alone tonight. I don't tell her I was in the middle of chugging hard alcohol from the bottle. I don't tell her that if she hadn't come over, by midnight I'd have passed out sitting up on the couch and woken up in the early morning in the same position. I want to hang out with her, but I have already tasted vodka. So I lie. She offers me a ride into St. Albert and, being the sweetheart she is, says she'll pick me up in the morning. I say thanks. She thanks me for the gift. We kiss. We leave.

I wake up. I'm in a bed. I don't know whose. I look around. It's my buddy's spare bedroom. I slept at Jared's house. I walk downstairs. I find some leftovers and chug. Weekend hangover healer. I try to remember the night. Another blackout. My stomach punches my intestines. I have no fight left. Grace calls me. She's on her way. When she picks me up, I smell of booze and cigars. I think someone brought cigars. I'm in a daze. I don't know where we are. I ask where we're going. Grace asks me the same question. She reminds me I said I had this day planned out. I say I forgot. We go to Smitty's diner for breakfast. I feel like a winner. At breakfast, Grace brings up Big Valley, a country jamboree in Camrose. Paranoia strikes. I ask if she's just excited to go because her ex will be there. I don't know if her ex will be there. She looks in my eyes in disbelief. She looks to see if I've lost my mind. She sees I have. Grace starts to cry and leaves the table. I finish reading the sports section of the newspaper and drink my coffee. Through the window I see her crying in her car. I feel nothing. I finish my coffee and pay the bill. I go to her car. I give my speech. I'm not receiving the usual feedback. My lies are receding. I'm the boy who cried wolf. It's raining hard. We rent some Anthony Hopkins movies. We lie in my bed. I feel sick. Grace has energy and wants to do something. That annoys me. I don't reply. My stomach punches with force. Karma's a bitch. The day is cut short. Grace leaves, sad.

I'm sprawled on my bed, motionless. It's been hours. I need energy to get downstairs. It's Sunday. Liquor store closes soon. I'm too hung over to drink. I pick myself up. I take the elevator to the foyer. I walk through the parking lot to the back cooler doors. I grab a bottle. I pay. I take my tunnel back upstairs. I sit on the couch. I don't care. I don't feel. I hate myself. I hate life. *You won't have to worry about that for too much longer.* "Do you really think I need you around anymore? I know I'm fucked. Let me dig my grave in peace." I search peace.

07/24/08, *Last Chance*

I'm trying to heal. I can't do this to Grace anymore. I love her. She's hurting. She hasn't given up. I don't know why. Her hope is stronger than mine. I'm doing a ten-day herbal detox. I tell people I'm cleaning my system. I'm running out of ways to eliminate alcohol. The detox doesn't allow alcohol or many foods. I've been eating Edo Japan's chicken, rice, and broccoli, with no sauce, for eight days. I didn't drink for the first three. Withdrawal kicked my ass. I gave up. Grace thinks I haven't had a drink for eight, which would be normal. I tried. I failed. Again. Tomorrow is Grace's friend's birthday. I said I'll cut the detox a day short to come see her. She said I can still see her and not drink. I said I might not. I will.

I pick up a case of beer for a friend at the party. I pick up a two-six for Grace and me. I get paranoid. It's not enough. I get a mickey of Smirnoff and a bottle of wine. I'll say it's for the party. I get to the party. Grace greets me. I see the resentment in her eyes. This can't be healed. Our tension is public. The night progresses. I get shitfaced. I black out. I wake up. Grace is beside me. Grace wakes up. Paranoia hits. A vision from the night appears in my head. Her friend was telling a joke. She laughed and touched his arm. I tell her that her flirting disgusted me. Grace is baffled. I'm baffled. She asks if I remember the night. I say yes. I don't. She asks if I remember flipping out on her in front of her friends and telling her she had issues. I say yes. I don't. I say it's true. I don't know why I say it's true. It's not. I have issues. She turns to stone. She tells me to leave. I tell her we're going to the Capital Ex amusement park today. We had it planned. She says we're not going. I tell her I'm sick of her resentment. She shakes her head. Grace looks at me. She tells me she can't do this anymore. That I should leave. I say I'll call her later. She tells me it's over. I shrug my shoulders. I say, "Fuck it."

I walk toward Jimmy. I throw Jimmy's keys against the fence. Jimmy's alarm breaks. I punch Jimmy. Jimmy has a dent. I drive a couple of blocks to Mom's. It's morning. I'm still half-cut. Luckily, she lives close. I don't want to drive to my apartment in Edmonton. I don't drive drunk. I guess now I do. Mom's in Hawaii with her friend. I go downstairs. Dave left beer. I grab a beer from the mini-fridge. I chug it. I grab two more beers. I go to the bathroom. I shotgun them. I go back to the mini-fridge and grab two more beers. Chug one. I chug half the other one and stop. I want to keep chugging, but my stomach is full of liquid. Beer is weak. I want a case of vodka.

I sit on the couch and watch TV. Mark calls me to go golfing with him, Darren, and Mike. I say if he's driving. I go golfing. After six holes, I quit golfing. I sit in the cart and drink. The sun is out. I only see dark clouds. I call Grace. She doesn't answer. I text her: "Sometimes a break is a good thing." Grace texts back: "This isn't a break Luke. I'm sorry." I curse. Mark tells me to stop calling her. I call her. No answer. I shotgun a beer with Darren and Mike. I go to the cart. I hide and chug another. I puke beer on the course. Mark looks at me in disgust. He's not impressed. He tells me this isn't the Luke he knows. I've let down a friend. He tells me to take it easy on the booze. I tell him it's not a big deal. I say it's the first day of a breakup—I'm supposed to get shitfaced. Mark drops me off. I keep drinking. I search peace.

"Luke?"

My name appears in my dream.

"Luke?"

I wake up.

"Luke, you shithead, wake up."

That's Tommy's voice. What's he doing here?

"Hold on." I get up and wrap up in my blanket. I walk to the TV room. "Hey." Did he sleep over?

Tommy looks at me and laughs.

"Wow, rough night?"

"It was my friend Karley's wedding. My parents are friends with her parents and were there with their dates. I sat between them at the church. I got shitfaced." I give him an excuse for my drinking. "But it was fun." I don't remember. "Did you stay over?"

He gives me a look of concern.

"Holy shit, Luke! I wasn't even with you last night. Remember we planned to watch football today?"

"Oh yeah." I don't remember. "How did you get in? Did you even call?"

"Dude, I called you over five times. You never answered. I was in your area so I thought I'd check to see if you were here. And for some reason your door was unlocked."

"Hmm. Sorry about that."

We watch football. I can't see straight. Images are blurred. I tell him I'm going to bed; he can stay and watch football. I tell him I'm sorry. I go to sleep. I wake up three hours later. Calm. Storm. Knives of a butcher carve. Axes swing with brutal force. Fists pummel with no remorse. Groan. Anger. Pain - second rush - Thunder. Jolts. Anger. Curse. Pain. Clench. Curse. I ate last night. I stumble to the bathroom. I puke up everything I ate. I crumble to the floor. I lie in a comatose state, motionless.

I haven't moved in hours. I've always thought about dying. I've never felt death. I've lived a permanent hangover. I've never felt death. I lift myself up. I feel death. I plop my head on the toilet seat. I puke bile sideways. It stains my cheek. My head slips from the toilet seat. It bounces off the tiles. Knockout punch. Time passes. I wake up. Death knocks. I keep myself awake. I shake my head. I attempt a second wind. I sit up. My head hits the toilet. My vision blurs. I keep my eyes open. I use my puke-stained toilet seat as leverage. I get up. I lean on the countertop. I look in the mirror. I see death. I stand. I feel death. I swallow. I wobble like a boxer on his last breath before the knockout punch. *Okay, Luke, I can't punish you much more. I'm going to give you two options. This is your last chance.* "Fuck off." *You have to trust yourself for the first time, come clean about your secret, and get help. If you chose option two, you will either die, or, if you're lucky, you will only be a dropout loser.* "Fuck off." *This is not a joke, Luke. This is your life.* "What life?" *I've been a hard-ass on you, because you need tough love to see your potential.* "You're a joke." *You can do this. But it can only happen if you admit defeat and get help.* My head bangs against the mirror. I lean on the mirror for support. I dry heave. No bile left. I stumble. I lean on the wall. I stand straight and balance myself. I stumble to my bedroom. I crumble to the floor. Time passes. My eyes open. It's dark outside. I feel the symptoms. The mistress is calling. My body shakes. Vodka's my only thought. I shiver. I need vodka. I'm cold. Vodka. I pick myself up. I wipe off the puke, change my shirt, spray cologne and grab a piece of gum. I take the elevator downstairs. I go get vodka. Only a mickey. I stumble to the couch. I open the bottle. Thirteen ounces. The smell makes me gag. I plug my nose and chug three ounces. I puke on my shirt. I plug my nose. I chug the remaining ten ounces. I hold my lips together and force my puke back. I need every ounce. I pass out.

I wake up. One word left. Death. I lift myself off the couch. I walk to the balcony windows. I lean my hands against the window to hold myself up. I stare into the sky. Light clouds surround the day. People are living. People are dying. People are happy. People are sad. I contemplate my life. Am I destined to die now? Is this how it ends? *I gave you the choices.* I stare blindly into the blue sky. Mindless time passes. I'm met with visions of family, the kids, and friends. Everyone is smiling. Why? Time passes. They smile. They know. I nod. They know who I am. The person I don't see. The potential I have. They know. I don't know. I want to know. I grab my phone. I collect myself. I breathe. I need a mask. I dial numbers.

"Son!" Mom is always cheerful.

"Hey, Mom." I speak as normally as possible. "What are you up to?"

"I'm just watching Oprah. What are you doing? How are you feeling from the other night?" She is referring to my blackout at Karley's wedding.

"Not bad."

"Do you remember me telling you to stop drinking? You got out of control."

"Yes, I do. I'm sorry." I don't remember.

"That's okay. You were fun, just overly drunk. I bet your hangover was enough punishment."

"It was." I'm happy she doesn't know the severity. "Can I stay with you for awhile? I don't want to be in my apartment right now. Too many memories of Grace." I use Grace as an excuse.

"Of course, Luke. I think it would be a good idea. You seem to be struggling."

"I am. Thank you. I will be over in a couple of hours."

"See you soon. I'm excited!" She brightens life. I darken it. I hang up. I clean myself up. I pack a bag. I drive to Mom's. *Good job, Luke. You're taking the first step.* "Seriously, fuck off. This is temporary. I'll prove to you I can drink." *You will fail.* "I can't get any worse." *You can and will get a lot worse, if you don't ask your mom for help.* "We'll see." I get to Mom's. I put on my strongest mask. We sit and talk. Mom tells me stories of when I was younger and we had conquered every obstacle to come our way. She tells me to be strong. She tells me to remember the strength I had as a child. I feel like a failure. I'm sickened to realize I had been stronger and happier as a kid at a time when I thought life couldn't get worse. I had conquered a disease that was given to me. Now, I'm dying from something I've given myself. I tell Mom I love her. I thank her for welcoming me. She says she couldn't be happier. We hug. Mom tells me she's going to Hawaii in two days. I don't want to keep her from her trip. I don't tell her I have a drinking problem.

09/10/08, Losing Hope

6:00 am

I'm home from driving Mom and her friend to the airport. I haven't had a drink for two days. I've been dealing with withdrawal in isolation. I sleep in the guest room in the basement. I don't let Mom see me suffer. Now that she's gone, I don't have to hide. Death is suffocating me. I shake. Paranoia is at its peak. I can't fight back with vodka. I won't let myself. I'm sitting on my bed. The room is black. I'm staring at darkness, in fear. I'm scared. I terrify myself. I know what I've become. I'm everything I hate. I can't drink. I stare at death. I rock back and forth. I shake. I sweat. I cry. I can't drink today. I have no one to stop me. I don't trust myself. I hope I die in an accident, so my death from alcohol won't be revealed. The secret will stay alive. Only I will perish. Lives will go on. Happiness will proceed. It'll be a favour from me. My life will be remembered full of dreams. People will cry because it happened too soon to a good person. Life will continue without the truth. That's all I want. I want my secret to live. Not me. I can't drink. I go have a shower. Tears fade into the water. I bang my head on the shower wall. I get out of the shower. Shakes take over my body. I crumble to the floor. I'm terrified. I have to go to school. I have an exam. I lie motionless on the tiles. I stare at the ceiling in defeat. It's hard to find that mask. I used to be a master. Now I suffer. I wish I had been busted. I wish Grace had busted me. I wish she was beside me. I would recover. Now I suffer.

6:00 pm

I don't work tonight. I have been given a two-week leave. My supervisors and the kids' parents are worried about me. They feel I have lost emotion. They don't see my usual excited self anymore. They know me best. I see the families the most. They care for me. They worry. I sat down with my supervisors. They worry too. I say I haven't dealt well with a breakup. I don't tell them that alcohol has possessed my life. I don't tell them I've almost completed self-destruction. I don't tell them I've dug my grave. I don't tell them it's waiting for my arrival. I want to tell them, but I don't. I almost break down. I swallow back weakness. They see my fear. They tell me that it's okay. They tell me to take some time off to care for myself. I ask if I'm fired. They reassure me I'm great at what I do. They don't want to lose me. They want me to work on my personal life, so I can help the children. I agree.

I took that time to end up on the bathroom floor. I called to ask for more time. I'll work next week. I'm watching football. Colts are winning. I'm not cheering. I see, hear, and feel booze. I get up. I go to the liquor store. I have a paper due tomorrow. I haven't started. I can't hold off. I get back. I start my paper. I open the bottle. I write. I drink. *Luke, what the hell?* "Now you show up?" *When you don't drink, I leave you alone. You have to take the first step alone. I can only push you.* "I've had the first taste. I feel great. Grace is dating her ex. I'm happy for her." *You don't know that, and who cares if she is? You better not be drinking because of that. You're hopeless, Luke. You're the ex now. Get over it.* I take a swig. I finish the paper. The topic is anti-depressants. I say they're a marketing scam. I say there's no point in ten years of post-secondary education to work with the mind, when you can hand out drugs for something that can be healed through therapy. I say they can be useful temporarily, but they are not the solution. I say alcohol is just as effective. I say they both repress memories. I say alcohol is more fun. I say it's a continuous dance with the devil. I delete the last two sentences. I go downstairs. I watch the NFL Network. I finish the bottle. I go to bed. I pass out.

10:00 am

I wake up. It's Thursday. I haven't gone to school since I handed in my paper. It's useless. I'm hopeless. I lie in bed for hours. I deal with mourning. I mean morning. I numb my withdrawal symptoms. I get up. I eat. I puke what I eat. I watch TV. I can't focus. My body wants a drink. I want to drink. There's no life. I have no life. Only alcohol. Alcohol. I need alcohol. I hold off till early evening. A couple of friends call to hang out. I don't answer. I can't. My mask has faded. I can't lie anymore. I don't have it in me. I hate myself. I don't have coherent thoughts. They aren't coherent, because there are none. People talk to me; I don't hear them. Life is mute. A fog. A daze. People see me; I don't see them. A tunnel. Hollow. Dark. I stare at objects, and I don't think. Empty. Lost. Finished. Somehow, I'm in school. I'm passing. I don't plan to make it to the end of the semester. I'll have dropped out. Or I'll be dead.

2:00 pm

Mom called to tell me Aunt Danielle is coming in from Hong Kong to visit. She's coming tonight. I sigh with relief. I hesitate with fear. She'll protect me from vodka. I can't be without vodka. Mom's coming home tomorrow. I'm picking up my aunt at the airport at five. Do I buy alcohol now? *Luke, you have to tell your aunt. This is not an option anymore. Have you looked at yourself lately?* "I don't look in the mirror." *This is it, Luke. Do you want to be a psychologist? Do you want to help kids? You let go, and you selfishly give up on everybody. Those little guys you have taught, and who look up to you, smile when you arrive; they're eager to learn. You ready to lose that?* "Don't pull that shit on me. This is my life. Someone better will replace me. They'll be happy." *Those kids love you, Luke. The families love you. They go out of their way to praise you to your supervisors. You will break their hearts.* "People quit. People die. Life goes on." *What about your parents? The two people in your life that have done everything for you. You came into the world broken, and they fixed you. Do you know the impact it will have on them knowing they lost a son because he broke himself in secrecy?* "I'll die in a tragic accident." *What about your brother? He would take a bullet for you. Your relatives? The ones who helped you through your childhood. Your friends? The few people who have always had your back. Fuck, Luke, wake up!* "The world is better off without me." *The world needs you.*

7:00 pm

Aunt Danielle and I are sitting on the couch, talking. She's telling me stories. I don't know what she's saying. I want alcohol. I never see Aunt D. She lives across the world. She's my godmother. I trust her. She loves me a lot.

I cut her off.

"Aunt Danielle." Her last word was *shoes*. I'm content not listening.

"Yes, Luke."

I pause.

"I have to tell you something." Emotions overwhelm me. My eyes swell.

She sees my fear.

"Sure, Luke, you can tell me anything."

That's it, Luke. You can do it. Come on buddy. I can't do this.

"Umm. No I can't."

I don't fool her. She sees severity.

"That's okay, Luke. You don't have to tell me anything you don't want to." She sits patiently.

I breathe. I slowly put my head in my hands. I close my eyes. I see death. I open my eyes. I look at Aunt Danielle.

"I have a drinking problem." Tears cover my cheeks. I don't make a sound. I'm stone in a rainstorm. I'm terrified.

Aunt Danielle looks confused. Not her little Luke. Not her godson. Not the boy who wants to be a doctor. Not the boy with ambitions and dreams.

"Are you sure, Luke?"

"Unfortunately," I muster out.

"How long have you thought you had a problem?"

"It's not what I think, Aunt Danielle. If it was, I could have fixed it. I'm an alcoholic. It's been years." Truth leaves my mouth. I haven't spoken the truth in reference to myself since I picked up that first drink in secrecy.

She doesn't comprehend.

"When was the last time you drank?"

"Last night and every night before that. No one knows. If I don't get help now, I'm done. I wrote a paper drunk last week. I've written ninety percent of my exams on hangovers. It's the reason I lost Grace. I'm on leave from work. My supervisors told me to take time off. I quit boxing. I told Mom I wanted to stay here because I needed a change of environment. It was really because last weekend I gave myself a choice to live or die. I didn't drink the two days we were here together. When Mom left for Hawaii, I drank. I tried not to. I have no control. I can't live with myself anymore, Aunt Danielle. I live a lie. I'm a bad fucking person." I drop my head.

Aunt Danielle grabs me in her arms. She sings a French tune. Her soothing voice comforts me. She stops singing to speak.

"You asked for help, Luke. Everything will be better from now on. I promise you." The Falardeau sisters are strong.

"Anything will be better." *You did it, Luke. You don't need me anymore.* "Thank you."

Aunt Danielle tells me she has faith in my recovery. I say I need to find faith. We hug. I say good night. She tells me she loves me and is proud of me. I've lost pride. I tell her I love her. I go to bed. I feel safe. I feel scared. I feel sick. I go puke. I shower. I go to bed. I sleep sober.

Day Two

I wake up. I shake-shit-shower-shave. I fight pain. I ask Aunt Danielle to help me tell Mom. I tell her this is hard. She says the best things in life come from hard work. Mom gets home late. We sit her down. I tell her. Her expression matches Aunt Danielle's. She asks the same questions. She embraces me with tears. She's proud of me. I don't feel pride. She supports me. She asks if I'm ready to go to AA. I say yes. It's late. We will set it up for tomorrow. I feel like a child taking his first steps. I don't like that feeling. I'm twenty-three.

09/20/08, AA

Friends want to see Aunt Danielle. There's a big table for us at
Sorrentino's. I don't want to see Grace. I go to Sorrentino's. Grace
isn't working. I order a pop. I notice Aunt Danielle looking at me.
We make eye contact. She looks scared, but hopeful. She smiles with
a sense of sorrow and pride. I smile back, taking in her strength.
Mom secretly tells me where the AA meeting is. I leave early to go to
the meeting. Mom walks me outside. She asks if I want her to come.
I tell her I need to do this on my own. I thank her for her support.
We hug. She tells me she loves me. A tear forms beneath my left eye.
I nod. A tear falls on my cheek. Mom wipes it away. I smile. I turn
and walk toward Jimmy. Dark clouds cover the sky. Tears trickle
from the clouds. I've never been more terrified in my life.

7:50 pm

I park Jimmy next to an old Buick. The rain picks up. I walk toward
the building. My heart pounds. I try one door. It's locked. Raindrops
drip off my hair onto my face. I try the second door. It's locked. I
hope it's cancelled. I walk to a third door. It opens. A wise-looking
old man turns his head. He looks confused. Within seconds, he
knows. He sees my broken spirit.

"Hey, son. Are you here for the AA meeting?"

I nod. I have no words hearing that question for the first time.

"It's at the end of the hall to your left."

I smile.

He smiles back.

The building is empty. I feel hollow. I feel sick. I follow my
footsteps. I walk into an old classroom. There are only old people.
I want to make sure I'm in the right place. I don't want to mention

AA. I'm embarrassed. I'm ashamed. I walk up to a lady in her mid-forties. She looks gentle. This can't be AA. These people look happy.

"Is this the place?" I softly mumble.

"What place?" I could be a punk. It's anonymous. We stare into each other's eyes.

"AA?"

"Yes. Welcome. What's your name?"

"Luke." We shake hands.

"Hi, Luke, I'm Jane. Is this your first meeting?" She sees the shattered pieces.

"Yes, it is."

"Oh, well, let's get you started. Come here for a second."

I follow Jane to the front of the class. She goes into a closet. She comes out with a big book.

"Here you go, Luke. Don't feel pressure to read any of this, but when you get some time or feel like drinking, read *Alcoholics Anonymous*. It might help you out."

"Great. How much do I owe you?"

"It's on us." Jane smiles.

I feel welcomed.

"You are very kind."

"It's our pleasure. If you want to take a seat, we'll get started."

"Thank you."

I sit in the back corner. I listen. I sense doubt. They ask if new members want to identify themselves. I sit passively. When it's over I'm the first one out. I speed-walk to Jimmy. I crank my tunes. I bang my head against the steering wheel. "Fuck!" I'm not like these people. I know I have a problem, but I can't be like them. I close my eyes. I see death. I open my eyes. A tear falls on my cheek. Anger fills my soul. How did I get here?

Day Four

Withdrawal sucks. It can be healed with one thing. Alcohol. That one thing will kill me. Vicious cycle. Mom, Aunt Danielle, and two close friends, Britt and Ben, know I'm an alcoholic. They keep secrets. I trust them. I want to tell Grace. I'm scared to tell Grace. I don't want to tell Grace. I have to tell her. She deserves to know. She's better off not knowing. I attend another meeting. I don't talk in meetings. I sit in the back corner. I listen. I'm not like them. They went through worse shit. I'm young. They're old. I don't want to quit. I'll take a sabbatical from drinking.

Day Five

Fucking shakes, pains, cold sweats. Fucking thoughts, memories, life. I attend another meeting. I write Grace a long letter. I try to explain I'm an alcoholic. I don't know how it's possible for her to believe me. It can't be possible through her eyes. She would have known. Grace is smart. She's going to be a chartered accountant. I enjoyed her intellect.

Day Six

Physical pain is weak. Emotional pain is powerful. A drink will ease my mind. Thirteen drinks will relieve my thoughts. Twenty-six drinks will eliminate my thoughts. I go to another meeting. Grace hasn't replied. I expected it. It sucks. I don't like living at Mom's. I love her, but I haven't been told what to do since I was sixteen. I do chores of my own will. I did. I want my independence back. I don't deserve it. I don't trust myself.

Day Seven

Grace hasn't replied. She has to hate me. I'm a monster. I shake, I get cold, I cry. Pain, sweat, tears. I'm in a constant battle with my stomach. It won't give up. It wants a drink. My body is allergic to it.

I didn't go to AA today. Don't need it. It's my cousin's wedding in Calgary tomorrow. I have a midterm on Monday. I told Mom that. She said I need company right now. She's right; I can't be alone. I said I'll go to the wedding.

Day Eight

I don't go to AA anymore. I'm not an alcoholic. My thoughts obsess over alcohol. My body craves alcohol. I'm not an alcoholic. I can't be. I'm young. I want to drink one day. I can drink one day. I told Mom I'm ready to move back home to my apartment. She says I should stay a little longer. My intestines hate me. I hate life. I'm off to watch two people join their lives together in happy matrimony.

Day Nine

I'm back in St. Albert. No word from Grace. I hope she hates me. It would be better than her hurting. Resentment is easier than pain. I don't want to take away her perception that we're not meant to be. It's better her thinking that than knowing there was a reason. I'm a bad person. That's the reason. She knows that. I'm explaining the obvious.

Day Ten

Grace won't reply. The fog is clearing. I feel a bit better. I went for a run. First time I exercised in months. I want to go back to boxing. I want to join the amateur team. I want to start fighting. But I quit boxing twice already. I don't think my trainer is impressed with me. I got a personal trainer a few months ago. Then I quit with only a couple of sessions left. I didn't say why. I'm sure if I told him what happened he would understand. He's a boxer. I like boxing. I don't street fight. I box. I'll go back tomorrow. It'll make me happy.

Day Eleven

Grace isn't going to reply. I'm okay with that. My marks in school are getting better. I've attended class for a week straight. I started work. The kids don't see my pain anymore. They can read me better than anyone. They saw my hurt before, and it hurt them to know I was hurting. I'm happy they don't have to hurt for me anymore. I joined Panther again. My trainer was supportive and is happy I'm back. He tells me lots of boxers are there to stay clean from an addiction or to get out of bad environments. It's a good sport for our type. We take out our aggression through sport. It's a sport that allows us to fight with no consequences. I joined the amateur team. I'm feeling better. I've moved back to my apartment. I spend time in St. Albert to run errands for Mom. I'm having people over to party tonight. Then we're going to a bar on Whyte Avenue. I'm not going to drink. I told my friends I'm focusing on school.

Day Twelve

I shouldn't have put myself through temptation. I didn't enjoy last night. Everyone got drunk. Drunk people annoy me. I couldn't sleep. I haven't slept well since I moved back to Whyte. I doubt myself. I went to boxing today. I lost skill. I hope it comes back with sobriety. School's going good. Work's good. Grace and I don't talk. I don't think we ever will.

Day Thirteen

I watched football for the first time without a hangover. It's more enjoyable.

Day Fourteen

I saw Grace at school. She was walking with her ex. I should go to AA tonight.

Day Fifteen

I didn't go to AA last night. Dad is home from Hawaii. I'm meeting him at Sorrentino's for dinner. He doesn't know about my secret sobriety. I plan to tell him tonight. I hope Grace isn't working.

Day Sixteen

Grace was working last night. We made eye contact when I walked in. She looked down. I kept walking. Dad and I talked. I ordered water. I told him I'm taking a break from drinking. He said it was a good idea, after seeing the way I was drinking at Karley's wedding. He asked if I remembered the night of the wedding. I said yes. I didn't. He asked if I remember him being upset with me for being overly drunk. I said yes. I didn't. He asked if I had quit drinking after he left the reception. He had had an early flight to Hawaii in the morning and he'd asked me to stop drinking. I said yes. I doubt I stopped. I didn't know he'd left early. He said that was good. He spoke to me about Uncle Gary and his drinking. I miss Uncle Gary. I hate sobriety.

Day Twenty-three

I'm still sober. I haven't been to AA. My intestines are still pissed. I'm not healing. School, work, and boxing are going well. I still think of Grace every day. I wish she would talk to me. I could get over it. She doesn't talk to me. I understand. Maybe she didn't understand my letter. Maybe I should send her another one explaining it better. I'll write Grace an email.

Day Twenty-four

Grace didn't answer. I think she understood the first one. Maybe she thinks I'm getting sober as an excuse to get her back. Am I?

Day Thirty

A friend told me Grace is dating her ex. I had already come to that conclusion. I wasn't mad. I pushed her to him. She's living through what I created. I'm not surprised. I'm not happy, but I expected it. I'm not getting sober for her. This is for me. I sparred today. I did well. I have nothing to lose. So I don't. My stomach pains come and go. I got a few Bs on a few assignments. I want As. Work's progressing. The kids are doing great. I'm regaining my life. I think I might want a girlfriend. I haven't gone on a date, let alone kissed a girl, since Grace. Instead of finding a rebound, I'd get shitfaced alone. Now I'm sober. I should date. I don't want to. I want Grace. Fuck, am I serious? She's dating her ex. I'm the ex now. I need to move on. I didn't go to AA. I'm still on a sabbatical. I miss alcohol.

Day Thirty-eight

The past week has been boring. Excitement has vanished. Reality bores me. It's filled with pain. It's Halloween. My friends and I are going to the Halloween Howler at the Shaw Conference Centre downtown. I'm driving. I say I'm focusing on school. I'm lying about the real reason I'm sober. I'm ashamed. Alcoholics are failures. Rehabs are for quitters. I have a bear costume. I went on a date with this girl. She's not for me; I'm not for her. She gave me a bear costume.

Day Thirty-nine

I didn't like the Howler. Everyone was drunk. Drunk people don't make sense. I should go to AA. It's a friend's birthday tonight. We're going to Japanese Village. I like Japanese Village. Tonight I'm not drinking, because I have a test on Monday. I don't. Another sobriety lie. I thought I'd stop lying when I got sober.

The Next Day

I wake up. Calm. Thunder. Lightning. Axes. Storm. Knives. Battle. Punches. Defeat. I grimace in pain. I drank last night. I walk to the bathroom. I puke. At Japanese Village, I had a Pepsi and a green tea. After Japanese Village, everyone decided to go to a bar. I said I was going home to study. I said my goodbyes. At dinner, I had decided I was going to drink when I got home. I told myself during that dinner that I wasn't an alcoholic. I told myself that when I got home I was going to drink that bottle of wine Lisa had left behind a couple of weeks ago. It never tempted me. It's sparkling wine or some girly shit. She had told me to chuck it. I kept it. I told myself that I was going to have one glass of awful-tasting alcohol and not drink for two weeks. I heard someone say in AA that if you don't think you're an alcoholic, you should go out and have one drink with what has been said in AA in the back of your mind.

After I had a sip of the sparkling pink wine, I grimaced. I glared at the bottle. I looked at the time on the stove. I went back to watching TV. Not knowing what I was watching, I looked at the time again. Two minutes had passed. I looked at the bottle. I grabbed it. I chugged half the bottle. I grimaced. I finished the bottle. I felt rejuvenated. It was getting late. I ran the stairs down to the liquor store like a little boy on Christmas morning. I grabbed a mickey of beautiful Alberta Pure and a delicious nine-dollar bottle of wine. I ran back up the stairs. It was bliss. The devil herself joined me for a dance. And we danced the night away. I loved it. My mind came in at times, but the mistress and I shrugged it off, and we laughed and laughed and laughed.

Now I'm reflecting on my delusional thoughts. Last night was depressing. I proved I was an alcoholic. I am an alcoholic. I'm the most miserable I've been in my life. While drinking from the bottle, I sat there motionless. I stared down the wall. Turns out I'm fucked. I have run out of ifs ands or buts. I'm an alcoholic. I can still keep it a secret. Mom travels enough for me to put on masks. Ben and Britt know about my drinking, but I won't drink when out with the boys. Aunt Danielle is across the world, and Grace doesn't talk to me. I'll stay on a sabbatical in others' eyes, so news can't get to any of the previously mentioned people. I'm scared. My capabilities of deception are terrifying. Alcohol is my number-one priority. I should go straight to AA. I don't want AA. I want alcohol. Beautiful, miserable alcohol. My mistress. The dance with the devil continues.

Next Day

I cancelled work for the rest of the week, prolonging the inevitable. I don't want the little men to see my pain. They're better off without me. I'll quit work soon. Get that one out of the way. No more worry for the families about my condition of self-destruction. I went to boxing today. I felt like shit. I don't know if I did something to my left arm. I hope it's only a pinched nerve. Half of my left arm is consistently numb. I tried to hold a schoolbook tonight while I was studying/drinking. My arm fell asleep within twenty seconds. I got scared. I let go of the book. I stopped studying. I continued to drink. I don't care. This slip, as they call it in AA, shows me who I'm supposed to be. I'm a nobody. I'm an alcoholic. A freak. An outcast. Destined to lose. I hate losing. I hate myself. You won't hear from the voice in the back of my mind. It gave up on me, when I gave up on myself. I have no thoughts, emotions, or feelings toward life. I live in a tunnel. I'm quitting it all. Fuck school. I can't pass, when I'm a drunk. Fuck it. I aim for the gutter. I search peace.

Next Day

I go to boxing. I spar. My left arm is numb throughout. It's hard to throw jabs, because I don't have feeling behind the punch. I don't show weakness. Instead, I box like a pansy, mostly defending myself. I get beat up pretty good. I have to let go of boxing again. This time for good. The second-last lose. I'm all that's left.

I'm on my way home, with a pounding head and a cut lip, when Tommy calls. He asks if I'm going to watch the Oilers' game. I say yes. He says he'll come over. As I hang up, I see Grace and her ex—

now boyfriend—walking on the sidewalk in my neighbourhood. It's 7:00 pm. I think I'm hallucinating. I have my glasses on for driving at night. It's Grace and Steve. What is she doing two blocks from my place? They live in St. Albert. I live in Edmonton, in the south end. It's near the university, but they're coming from an apartment building. Maybe it's a friend's place. Anger builds inside me. My right fist tightens. My left hand grips the steering wheel. My heart pounds. My teeth clench. I want to drop him. I want to turn back and kick his ass. I don't. I take a deep breath. I remind myself it's my fault. He's happy I fucked up. I would be, too, in his shoes. I go to the liquor store. I get a bottle. I go to my apartment. I sit on the couch. I drink. I remember Tommy said he was coming to watch the game. I curse. I hide the bottle. He comes over. We watch the game. I take bathroom breaks to swig vodka. I tell him about seeing Grace. I tell him I got shit-kicked. He says I'm hallucinating or have a concussion from sparring. I tell him I didn't get knocked out, just dazed. I saw what I saw. He said who cares if I did. I don't say anything. I shouldn't care. After the game, he leaves. I continue the dance.

Next Day

I wake up on the floor by the TV. I lie on my back. I stare at the ceiling. I ride out morning withdrawal. Hours pass. I can't live here anymore. I'm trapped in this capsule. I've lost my one place of solidarity. Paranoia. Pain. Fear. Anxiety. Withdrawal. Gut. Anger—so much fucking anger!—Paranoia. Terrorists. Spies. Fear. My liquor store isn't mine anymore. The news has spread. The world knows. Her friends are all over the place. People call me. I don't answer. My cover is blown. I don't go to school. I don't go to work. I don't box. I don't speak to the African man. I go in, grab vodka, look down, pay exact change, and walk out. I speed-walk to my apartment. I take the stairs, lock the door, sit on the couch, and drink. My numbness has spread to my left leg. I don't know what it is. It's consistently numb, like my arm. Who gives a shit? It's part of the final loss. I drink. I search peace.

Next Day

I wake up. I ride out morning withdrawal. Hours pass. I pack a bag. Mom's in Hawaii. I'm going to her house. I like it better. It has more space. It's clean. Buddies are close. I have to be careful living in St. Albert. It's a soap opera. Everyone knows everything about everyone. Like a bubble. The only way to dodge the gossip is to hide from everyone. I expose myself enough to show normality and a picture of an ambitious student. People don't know I'm taking time off work. People don't know I don't show up for class. Most people don't know I ever boxed. I keep a low profile. Friends come over in the late afternoon. We play Wii. At 6:00 pm I feel the symptoms. I tell them I have to get my study on. Big test coming up. I tell them school is easy on this sabbatical. They leave. I wait ten minutes. I leave to go buy vodka. Now I drink. I'm tired of this process. I'm sick of this process. I chug. I pass out.

Next Day

I feel death.

Next Day

I welcome death.

Next Day

The devil moves in.

Next Day

Our battle continues.

Next Day

I fight death.

Next Day

I'm on the bathroom floor.

Next Day

I admit defeat.

Next Day

I search peace.

Next Day

I need help.

Next Day

I want help.

Next Day

Mom's coming home tomorrow. I'm digging for clarity. I need my mind to help me back to recovery. *What is it, Luke?* "Oh, thank God. I need to get help. I'm serious this time." *Luke, you're at your rock bottom.* "I know I am." *One more week of this, you lose it all. You keep drinking, you drop out of school and lose your job. Then you have to spill the secret, because you will become a nobody. A disgrace to your family name.* "I know. I know." *When your Mom gets home tomorrow, you go to AA. You don't break her heart and let her know you slipped. You pull out a tough front and show you are doing well through recovery.* "I will." *You go to AA, and you stay in AA.* "Okay." *You can never drink again.*

Where I Am Now

We admitted we were powerless over alcohol—that our lives had become unmanageable.

Who cares to admit complete defeat? Admission of powerlessness is the first step in liberation. Relation of humility to sobriety. Mental obsession plus physical allergy. Why must every AA hit bottom?

Twelve Steps and Twelve Traditions

November 20 '08

Mom is proud of me for staying sober. I want to tell her the truth. I go to AA. I sit at the table. I listen. One man had a shotgun to his head. Another had sporadic alcohol-induced seizures for a decade. Another ended up in a mental institution. Another was there by court order and hated us. Another saw his mom get shot and killed at three, and was raped at five. Another wants to commit suicide, and he cried. I'm there in secret. I'm scared.

November 21 '08

I wake up. I'm sick. I know the pain is weakness leaving my body. I go to school. It's Friday. I go to AA. I go home. I'm staying in. I'm terrified of the outdoors. I'll end up in a liquor store. I don't trust myself. I watch the NFL Network.

November 22 '08

I wake up. I shake. I eat breakfast. I have one bite. My stomach cuts my intestines. I go for a run. I last twenty minutes. My stomach is nauseous. I have cold sweats. I go to AA. I'm asked to talk. I politely say no thank you. I listen. "God Grant Me the Serenity to Accept the Things I Cannot Change, the Courage to Change the Things I Can, and the Wisdom to Know the Difference." I don't believe in God.

November 23 '08

It's Sunday. Sunday Night Football. Colts versus Chargers. I sacrifice. I go to AA. I cover my face while I'm walking to the church. The bubble can't find out. I'm asked to speak. I do. I say, "Hi, my name is Luke. I'm an alcoholic and, ironically, a five-year psychology student." They laugh with me. I laugh at myself. The topic is alcohol as a number-one priority. I tell them a story of when Grace and I got into a fight. I was hung over, as always. I was rude, as always. I made her cry, as always. She left my place sad and confused, as always. She called later to make up. We went for dinner. She bought me a gift and a card that said she loved me. The gift was a movie, *Semi-Pro*. She wanted to watch it. I remembered I didn't have alcohol at home. We were in separate vehicles. I said, "Sure, I'll meet you at my place." I picked up booze and I hid it. I met Grace at the front doors. The night went on. Symptoms made their way to my body. I needed to drink, so I started a fight with Grace. She left crying. I drank. I ask what the other topic is. They say consciousness. I say I'm looking forward to regaining it.

November 24 '08

I'm starting to recover. I live with physical pain. That's okay. The emotional weight is not as heavy. My shoulders are feeling loose. Colts won last night. I ran around the basement fist-pumping. A jolt of pain ended it. They're on a roll. I like that. I ran for half an hour. I went to school. I got a B+ on a paper I wrote sober. I'm improving. I worry I've ruined my chance for graduate school. I will keep trying. If I stay sober, anything is possible. I received average grades as a broken-down alcoholic. Anything is possible sober. I use the power of my mind in my favour now. I'm back at work. I still have my boxing membership. I went to apologize for leaving without notice. I said I want to take some time off while I recover. I said I won't commit again unless I'm serious. I try to rebuild trust with my trainer, Rob. He's big. I go to AA. Someone tells a story. After decades of drinking, he ended up motionless on the kitchen floor. He tried to get up. He couldn't. Eight hours later, his wife got home from work. She found him there. She had been going to AA. She stood over him and asked if he was ready. He was. His withdrawals were filled with weeks of hallucinations. I like his story. He sits with his wife every meeting. We don't relate to a great extent. But I like his story.

November 25 '08

The cloud is dissipating. My stomach still hurts. I'm not healthy. I'm trying. I went for a run. Half hour again. I still hide my alcoholism. I feel embarrassed. I feel like a failure. I'm ashamed of my existence. I go to AA. They tell me we aren't saints. We're human. We've trapped ourselves in a losing battle. They say admitting defeat has been our biggest victory. They say this while smiling and laughing. Real smiles. Real laughter. Maybe I am human. They say people coming out of church on Sundays aren't saints when they cheat on their spouses, build gambling debts, drive drunk, and so on. Everyone is human. AA is our place of comfort. We admit to our faults. We don't hide. I feel less abnormal. I still think rehab is for quitters. Now I think it's a good thing.

November 26 '08

I want to drink. I hate my life. This is too fucking hard. I can't control the pain. It hurts. I can't repress memories. They haunt me. I hate Grace for not talking to me. I go to AA. Someone mentions that as alcoholics we were selfish children. We would do anything for that next drink. We had put relationships second, after the bottle. We didn't care about others. We couldn't care for ourselves. We were losers. I don't hate Grace. I feel bad for Grace. I hate myself. I'm not going to drink. I'll let Will Power take over tonight. I need its help. I can't do it alone.

November 27 '08

I wake up early. I'm not hung-over. I'm happy I didn't drink last night. I thank Will Power. I tell it that if my last name was Power, I would name my kid Will—even if it was a girl. I feel refreshed. I didn't wake up to my stomach. I go upstairs and give Mom a big hug. I love her. I don't love myself. Only enough to stay sober. I go to AA. I ask to speak. I say I have a confession. I say I have to be honest. I say it's the only way I'll stay sober. I tell them about my slip. I tell them about my deception. I tell them that in all my eight years of drinking, no one knew I drank alone. No one suspected it. No one knew who I really was. I tell them that I have heard a few times that every alcoholic thinks he gets away with it but never does. I tell them I'm the exception rather than the rule. I tell them I hate it. I tell them I've lived a lie. I tell them I'm scared to tell people about my deception. I feel sick. My stomach knots. I tear up. I hold it back. I tell them I wrote my ex a letter after we broke up and I got sober, to explain my deception, my drinking. I tell them she hasn't replied. I tell them I don't want anyone to know I'm an alcoholic. I tell them I'm ashamed to be an alcoholic. I stop talking. After the meeting, the man with the story I liked came to talk to me. He told me to be strong. He told me truth will be my greatest healer. He told me truth eliminates the extra weight. He told me it takes a big man to admit a slip, and it takes a bigger man to come back to AA after a slip. He told me not to try to talk to my ex. He said I'm not ready yet. I thanked him for his wisdom. We shook hands. I went to Mom's. Now I'm sitting in the guest bedroom, writing. I feel good. I've been sober a week. I feel an ounce of pride.

November 28 '08

I wake up early. I go for an hour's run. I'm getting deep tissue massages to fix my left arm and leg. They think it's a pinched nerve in my arm. They say there's a lot of built-up scar tissue in my leg. Withdrawal isn't as bad this time. A short slip. No more shakes. I go to AA. The other young guy, in his late twenties, isn't there today. He received his one-month chip yesterday. He's covered in tattoos and piercings. His pants are low, his hat is sideways, his hair is bleached, and he swears. He's a nice contradiction to the elders. He stirs the pot. He says funny things only a few of us understand. I like him here. We talk a lot. It's Friday. Not a good day to miss a meeting. I hope he didn't give up.

November 29 '08

I wake up refreshed for work. I go to work. We share lots of laughs. We work hard on the goals. We make lots of progress. I say my goodbyes. Little buddy, Connor, thanks me. His mom thanks me. I thank them. I love my job. It reminds me why I do what I do. It's Saturday. I go to AA. It reminds me what will happen to me if I pick up that first drink. I'm staying in to write. I'm writing a personal thesis. I want to answer all my questions. I want to be a symbol of what can happen. I want people to know what I didn't know before they end up where I was. I want people to know there is help if they are where I was. I want people to see it can happen to anyone at any age. I will do that through sharing my experience. Writing reminds me of where I was, what happened, and where I am now. I'm focused.

December 8 '08

I haven't written in a few days. Recovery is time consuming. Lots of mistakes to fix. That guy with the tattoos and bleached hair still isn't at meetings. I wish him the best of luck.

December 9 '08

I want to tell Dad the truth. I went to Mom, because she's my best friend, and she's a recovering alcoholic. I hesitate to tell Dad, because he's my idol, and I feel I've disappointed him. I have to be sure I will never drink again. I have to be sure I'm an alcoholic. I have to be sure about AA. I go to AA. I listen intently. I study everyone. I observe them. I see in their eyes what I have been searching. Happiness. The few who are beating this addiction one day at a time. One guy said he's been in AA for many years. He said out of the fifteen or so regulars, six people are still here and five have committed suicide. He said they committed suicide because they never recovered. I'm ready. I pick a sponsor, Ross. The guy I talked about whose story I liked. When I first came to AA, they told me to listen to stories for a week or two and then make my decision as to who I wanted as my sponsor. I'm a young kid, rare in AA, with a story different than the rest, the members have been supportive and appreciative of my openness. A couple of members offered me their guidance in sponsorship. But in the end, I went up to Ross and asked him. He's a wicked guy, with a sweetheart wife. She greets me with a hug every day. I've met their kids at a couple of meetings. They are my age and younger. It's nice to see a family there together sharing smiles, through stories of pain and suffering, knowing it's all in the past. They're happy now. Their lives couldn't be better. Ross's story is inspirational. I've been to a few meetings where the guy who's having a birthday (years of sobriety) asks Ross to speak on his behalf, because his story is that intense. I like Ross. I look up to him. I like the stories of crazy lives ending with a smile. It's a rarity in this world. It's those people who take crises and turn them into opportunities. It's the ones who don't look at what they don't have but focus on what they do have. This man takes his stumbling blocks and turns them into stepping stones.

Through psychology books on individual disorders, sociology books on society's dysfunction, work experience, and living through the eyes of a broken-down alcoholic, I've come to see that society isn't hopeless, as I had once thought. Society just needs some understanding and therapy. Open-mindedness is the key to recovery. Acceptance is the cure.

December 10 '08

I go to AA. I look around at the twenty-plus familiar faces of strangers whom I like. They're all successful in their fight to stay sober. Some are here with over thirty years of sobriety. I've come to enjoy and appreciate this place. It's been long enough for me to make my assessment: you go to AA, you stay sober. These people don't know my last name, but they would do anything to make sure I stay sober. I like that. The topic of the day is sex. They ask me to talk. I laugh. I say I don't think they want to hear my sex stories. I say, for all I know they could be about their daughters. They laugh. They know I'm not serious. They're open-minded to my humour. I tell them stories. I tell them girls have thought I used them for sex, because when they would come over, we would fool around, and then I would ask them to leave. I tell them I didn't do it just because I wanted sex. I liked their company. But I liked the company of alcohol more. I look around. I see nods. They know about the mistress. I tell them about my ex. I tell them how we had a great sex life till paranoia kicked in. I look around. I see nods. They know about the paranoia. I tell them paranoia, jealousy, and insecurity ruined the relationship. I tell them I never possessed those traits before alcohol possessed my mind. I look around. I see nods. They know about broken relationships. They know about shattered selves. I feel comforted. I feel I belong. Near the end of the meeting, someone says that alcoholics only relate to alcoholics. She says that alcoholics don't relate to people who don't drink, because they don't know what it's like to drink. She says alcoholics don't relate to people that can drink, because we can't. She says people who choose not to drink and people who can drink don't know what it's like not being able to drink. I belong here. She continues. She says she liked my story. She says it's important to find a relationship within yourself before you can make anyone else happy. I nod. She continues. She says it's tough not getting involved with someone for the first year of sobriety.

I ... uh ... what? The fog is gone.

"Wow! What? No sex for a year?" I'm not supposed to cross-talk. Sometimes rules have to be broken.

"Yeah." She smiles at the thought of me just finding this out. "It's an AA suggestion to find a relationship within yourself before you can make someone else happy. This is established after completing the Twelve Steps. It ranges within a year." She lightens the mood with her humour: "There's always that personal relationship." She looks at the lady beside her. "Because it's always done right." The ladies in the room laugh. She's referring to masturbation.

I cringe.

"No sex or alcohol. So, it is a cult. I'm kidding, I'm kidding." They laugh.

"But, seriously, a year? No fooling around? No taking girls home from a bar … oh, wait … So, not even a kiss? Nothing? Not even a date?"

"No. Sorry, Luke."

I rub my face and pull at my hair. Some of the old men are red in the face from laughing.

My helpful source continues, "Not unless you're already in a relationship. If that's the case, there's Al-Anon for the affected member of the relationship. And we know you're not in a relationship." She holds in a giggle. It slips out.

These people are comedians. "I figure I've gone long enough already. You guys are something, you know that?" The old men are wiping tears, chuckling.

"But you're the experts," I sigh. I was considering asking this girl out from class. Not anymore.

"You will be very happy, once you find that relationship within yourself, Luke."

"Always done right, right?"

We laugh. It's a good thing I heard about this after my assessment. Did they say anything about strip clubs? Nah, I'm kidding.

December 11 '08

I'm ready to talk to Dad. I'm building courage. My heart skips a beat thinking about it. I feel I've let him down, but now I know that I'm fixing that problem and doing positive things with it. I'm creating my destiny. I'll show him that tonight, at our traditional Sunday dinner. Dave will be there. I'll kill two birds with one stone. That sounds a little harsh, sadistic almost. I'll just tell them both at the same time.

I just got back from dinner. Dave wasn't there. His Washington Foreskins, I mean Redskins, were on SNF, so he stayed at his place downtown to watch it. I felt relieved to tell Dad. I ran to his place in my Rocky gear. It's a good distance from Mom's, and there's a foot of snow, so I figure it's twice the work, doubling the distance in my head. I had planned to stop for dinner before running to the AA meeting. The conversation with Dad was harder than telling Grace and Mom together. He responded with the expected confusion, asking if I was sure. I told him some stories. He agreed I was sure.

After a heartfelt discussion, Dad lightened up the mood.

"So, that's where all that money went," he laughed.

I laughed, relieved that he was laughing. I told him, for the most part, the truth about the money. The excuses I made for needing money to buy booze. The next step will be to tell him about boarding school and how I put his twenty-five grand on the line weekly. He's going to wring my neck. Hopefully, it will end with a pat on the back in acknowledgement of my past craft ... yeah, right.

I don't tell Dad that I'm working off a debt to the bank. Near the brink of my drinking, a couple of buddies and I went to Vancouver for my five-year high school reunion. This was in late August, after the breakup. I was in severe depression and wearing the biggest mask I could manage, to hide my despair. Not a good time for a reunion. After a couple of days there, we moved the party to my parents' place in Kelowna that they rent out. We went to some bars, but I wasn't feeling it. I didn't want a rebound. I wanted to drink alone. There was a casino connected to the condo where we stayed. For a couple of summers in the past, I had been a blackjack dealer at a casino. I knew the game, and I like playing it. I would leave the bar early and go to the casino. The last night, I had a blackout. I had a grand left. I found out I reached my overdraft limit of fifteen hundred bucks, which is a lot for an alcoholic student. I had saved over fifteen hundred from work for that trip and for drinking when I got back to school. That night, I blew twenty-five hundred bucks. I had no clue. I went home the next day. My bank card was declined at the liquor store. I went to the bank and asked what was going on. The girl looked at me as if I were a nut and asked if I had had a good weekend. I asked why. She showed me my statement. In half-hour intervals, I had been taking out four hundred bucks at a time. Turns out I'm not a good blackjack player during blackouts. I went home and scrounged up some change to buy booze. After awhile, it was getting too hard to figure out a way to drink. This helped me give it up. Best money I've ever spent.

After dinner, Dad gave me a big hug and said he was proud of me. I'm looking forward to feeling pride. I ran to the meeting feeling another weight had been lifted. The final weight. I went home and slept like a baby. I didn't hide *Alcoholics Anonymous* after reading a passage before bed; I'm not ashamed anymore. I'm an addict. I'm not a monster. I'm not an outcast or an abnormal member of society. I'm an alcoholic who chooses to fight his addiction with his buddy Will Power. My name is Luke, and I'm a grateful recovering alcoholic. I'm living my life I've come to enjoy.

December 12 '08

One of my supervisors came to do a follow-up from our meeting to make sure I was on the right track. When she came by, I greeted her at the door. She told me I was looking better. After we'd worked with the child, as planned, she told me she was happy to have the old Luke back. I've been getting a lot of that lately. I like it. It tells me I was a good person before alcohol, and even during alcohol, in some people's eyes. Near the end, they all could tell I was suffering inside. But no one knew why. I had used Grace as an excuse. She was part of it, but alcohol was the main factor. If I'd been sober, I would have gotten over her within weeks, not months. At work, I had never let my self-torment affect my job, except when the alcohol eliminated my emotions—which was when I left—and now I'm back and kicking ass. The little dudes see the light in my eyes, and they feed off that. We have lots of fun and share many laughs. There's not much to say about work, other than it's where I belong right now in my life. I want to teach these three little guys till I get my own practice. But I can't talk about it. I have to just do it. Nike style. I will do everything I can to help these kids grow up to be the funny, intelligent, athletic, ladies' men they've already started to become. I mean gentlemen, of course.

December 13 '08

In AA they say you will find out who your friends are once you get sober. A lot of members lost all their friends, because they got to a point in their lives where the only people they hung out with were the regulars at a bar. Or their friends couldn't handle a sober friend. A lot of people in AA had to sacrifice friendships for their sobriety. I think that's heartbreaking. I think it's inspiring that it didn't break them. They got sober, and they stay that way—happy. I'm lucky. A couple of weeks ago, I started telling my close buddies. I asked them to keep it a secret and cover for me if people made the connection to my daily disappearances from 8:00 until 9:00 pm. But since I told Dad, I feel I have nothing left to hide. I'm open about it. I don't care who the person is. I see people a lot since I came out of hiding. They ask how I am. I say, "Great, thanks, I'm a recovering alcoholic." They laugh in disbelief. I laugh along. They stop laughing and ask if I'm serious. I say yes. I continue to laugh—at their expressions of doubt. I find it funny. A fun ice breaker. Then we chat. I'm happy with myself and content with being an addict. It's not such a bad thing. The overwhelming support from my friends and family has provided me with comfort. A couple of buddies who have very strong characters have told me it takes a big man to do what I'm doing. I'm a better friend sober. I can commit to being a good friend. I don't hide. I can hang out without worrying about getting the next drink. My friends kick ass. I would take a bullet for each and every one of them. It's a good thing none of us are in gangs, or I would reconsider that notion. One friend took a lot of my shit for a few years. But he always stuck by. He knew I was better than that. A true friend. Thanks, Tommy. My friends add a piece to the scattered pride puzzle. They soften the blow of alcoholism.

December 14 '08

There are friends, and then there is that one friend you grew up with. The best friend. Matt Boyd is my best friend. We were neighbours since we were one. He stood by my side throughout my childhood.

He didn't look at me differently, as the other kids did. He didn't get upset when my skin wouldn't let me leave the house. He's chill. I've told Matt everything. A decade ago, he was the only one I told that I was going to write a book about my childhood so that I could help others. He told me I could do it. He gives me strength. Matt has been in the States on a hockey scholarship in Wisconsin for the past couple of years. I made this assessment of Matt after reading a book called *Outliers,* by Malcolm Gladwell. Gladwell explains how success is achieved through opportunities. I believe Matt would be in the pros if he hadn't missed out on one opportunity: his date of birth. The Canadian eligibility cut-off for age-class hockey is January first. Since he was born in September, it put him back nine months of physical maturity, which, at preadolescence, is a huge deal. With his natural talent and better coaching from earlier scouting, he would have had a better shot. Check the birthdays of any pro hockey team. The majority will be born in the first three months of the year. Matt will still go pro.

Matt is home for Christmas. I wanted to tell him my story in person. The news has already spread. That's St. Albert. Everyone knows. Joel let me know his sister told him. I had gone thinking she would. Girls and their gossip. Matt called Joel to ask if it were true. Joel told him it was, although everyone is confused. When I told Matt, he reacted like the rest, in disbelief. I told him stories. He said there's no doubt I'm an alcoholic. He smiled. He said I must have been good at hiding it. I told him that was nothing to be proud of. He told me I'm sober now—that's plenty to be proud of. I said thanks. Best friends for life, buddy. Thanks for always having my back.

December 15 '08

Alcoholics are emotional. I've had enough of it. The tears shed before were from anger and fear. The tears shed now are for recovery and faith. I hope it ends soon. It comes sporadically. Luckily, I haven't been busted yet. When I watch *Intervention* now on TV, I tear up. I used to watch that show while drinking alone and think I didn't have a problem. I figured I was nothing like those people. No one knew what I was doing. They were overtly showing their addictions. They knew they had a problem, and everyone around them knew they had a problem. I would watch it and feel better about myself. I thought I was a saint, because I wasn't directly affecting people's lives. But, in reality, I was indirectly affecting people's lives through negativity, lies, and deceit. I used to think the intervention part was sappy and boring. I liked the start, when it was about the intensity and how they had gotten there. After the intervention, the addicts would go to treatment—some of them would recover, and a lot of them would relapse after treatment. And it's obvious why. They stayed locked in rehab - a place away from booze. That can't be compared to real life.

The only way to recover is to live the same life while eliminating individual triggers. Exposure to real life will help Will Power get accustomed to your new life. You'll know what to do to distract yourself when you pass a liquor store, or have people over, or go places with drinks around. Alcohol isn't like other addictions. It's socially accepted. It's the only legal drug. I don't think alcoholics need rehab for more than a month. I think it's good for detox, if needed. But if the person is going to recover, it's not going to happen through others' will or lock-up, because alcoholics will always find a way to get alcohol if they want it. And once they get out, they become overwhelmed with freedom and notice a liquor store on every corner. The success rate can't be high. Alcohol is everywhere. You have to accustom yourself to it, or you will live in isolation. You can only recover through your own will. With it, you will build self-reliance. Once self-reliance is achieved, you can use your spirituality, family, support group, and friends as your backup to sobriety. You have to rely on yourself before you can rely on others.

I don't believe alcoholism is a disease. Every addict had repressed memories that led to the drinking. Underlying factors lead to the self-inflicted addiction. I believe it may be genetic, but even then, I don't believe an alcoholic is something one is destined to be. We choose to voluntarily medicate ourselves with alcohol. Depression is the cause; alcohol is the crutch. We treat our depression with a depressant. Eczema is a disease. There's no control. Alcoholism is an addiction. Will Power is the control.

December 16 '08

I'm opening myself to faith. I'm building open-mindedness to the concept of a higher power, creative intelligence, and/or a spirit of the universe. I have read the Alcoholics Anonymous book and heard many stories in AA about God. A good proportion of people going into AA are agnostic. I'm an agnostic. This means I'm open to the concept of God, but I need some sort of theory or proof to get me to believe in a power greater than any human – a power greater than myself. I have a glimmer of faith, yet a whole lot of doubt. I'm stubborn.

December 17 '08

My old apartment is a dungeon. The apartment looks nice, but built-up memories of pass-outs, falls, pukes, a broken relationship, and the vibe of complete hopelessness haunt the place. I spend every extra minute of my days, up to about eighteen hours of work a day, to get this place done. I picked final exam time to move. I need it out of my mind. Alone, I clean and box up my things. I need to face the memories on my own. I can't look at them anymore. I gag when I walk in. The room smells nice, but the memories don't. Today a few of my buddies came by to help me move all the big stuff out. To them it looks like a sweet pad. If only they'd witnessed an ounce of the self-induced terror I experienced there. I expressed to them my need to get this done fast. We put it into high gear and got it done. I left that apartment—and left the devil behind, dancing alone in her delusions. I don't have a home yet. I broke my lease on the apartment. When I told Dad about my addiction, I told him I couldn't live there another night. It has "relapsed" written all over it. He more than willingly told me to ditch it. We put all my stuff in his garage and some at Mom's place. I'm living at Mom's till we find me a safe haven. I need at least a month of sobriety to trust myself again.

I don't need my own place right now. It's not like I'm having sex. I'm a born-again virgin in more ways than one. The only difference is that with one of them (sex), I plan to lose my virginity one day. For the other (alcohol), I will keep the chastity belt on forever.

December 18 '08

Grandpa Dick's a stud. He's my Dad's dad. He played hockey for the USC Trojans on a scholarship in his prime. He also dated and married Miss North Carolina, Grandma Becky. She passed away eleven days before my birth. He fought in World War II as an American citizen. At one point, he was asked to try out for the Montreal Canadiens. He declined, because Grandma Becky and Gramps wanted a big family. They came home to Edmonton. They had eleven children. Gramps started a kids' clothing store called Jack and Jill. He supported his family. Gramps and Uncle Gary were best friends. Uncle Gary had been his only kid without a spouse. Uncle Gary lived in a single apartment, close to Grandpa Dick. They hung out every day. Grandpa's taking his death the hardest. He had no idea about Uncle Gary's alcoholism and is blaming himself. I went to see him today. I told him I'm a recovering alcoholic. He was in disbelief. I told him stories. I told him Uncle Gary's death helped get me sober. He cried. He hugged me. I hugged him back. He's proud of me. I'm still searching for pride.

December 19 '08

I sat down with Mom today and told her about my slip. She smiled and said she's glad I told her. She said she was worried about me back at my apartment. She said she's glad to have me at her house to help her during her recovery from surgery. She pretends she still can't lift over ten pounds. I laugh when she asks me to carry the toilet paper rolls. I tell her its one pound. She pretends to have back spasms. Back spasms aren't a side effect from her medications or surgery. I carry the toilet paper rolls, all six of them. She laughs. I love her.

December 20 '08

One month sober! Wicked! I feel great. I'm finishing up school and kicking ass doing it. Work couldn't be better. I look forward to work. Just as before the addiction took over my life, I don't consider what I do "work". It's my passion. It's my time to chill with hilarious dudes after studying. I've lost fifteen pounds of hooch fat. My immune system is strong. My stomach pains are gone completely. My mind is clear. I'm not stressed anymore. I take one day at a time and focus on the now. I'm really starting to enjoy my life. I have it pretty damn good.

One day I was sitting in a class, bitching to myself, knowing I could never drink again. Then we watched a movie about street kids in developing countries living a fulfilled life by finding happiness with what they have. They defined true happiness. I felt guilty for my previous self-pity. That was two weeks into sobriety. I haven't bitched to myself about not drinking since.

I still have times of cravings, but I'm working through that. When I do have cravings and pull a Tommy Gavin (Denis Leary, from *Rescue Me*) by walking past a bar or liquor store and finding myself stopping to stare in and daydream, I redirect my attention to my goal: finding meaning within my life. Or as Socrates said, "The unexamined life is not worth living." To take that journey, I have to stay sober. Another big thing that has helped me is a psychological treatment I gave myself. It's like classical conditioning. You know Pavlov and his dog; he shows how exposure to unconditioned stimuli, like meat, will create an unconditioned reflex: salivation. A conditioned stimuli is learned behaviour through association, say a food dish for eating the meat. Once this is paired significantly, the conditioned stimuli (food dish) will create a conditioned reflex (salivation) without the food being present. I've created an aversion to alcohol using that logic. I remind myself of the bad memories associated with alcohol and only the bad memories (conditioned stimuli): the days lying on the bathroom floor, the chugging and puking, the blackouts, the intense stomach pains, the losses, the misery. I've built such a strong aversion that if I look at, smell, or even think about alcohol during cravings, I gag. The gagging is my conditioned reflex.

A month of sobriety, and the pieces to the puzzle are starting to connect. Life is good.

December 21 '08

Autism: the mysterious disorder. The *who, what, how.* The unexplained. No etiology. No clue. Autism tears families apart. Autism brings families together. Autism causes stress. Autism creates joy. All we can do is treat the affected. Sociologists complain about psychologists, because they don't prevent issues, they only treat the already affected. If sociologists could prevent or find any answers, psychologists would be happily out of a job. But they haven't. Some things can't be prevented. Psychology works with the now. We work hard. We work to make the families' lives as easy as possible through extensive research and trial and error. Autism needs awareness. Autism needs acceptance. We're so focused on our own lives that if a child has tantrums in public we judge and think the parent is bad. We don't look beyond the problem. We don't know the pain, suffering, and time most of these well-educated parents have put into helping their children. If all the parents are like the ones I work with, then there's a reason why they were given children with autism: they're the strongest. Their intellect and confidence helps us find answers. We'll find answers. Autism will be treated. We're smart.

December 23 '08

Tonight wasn't cool. I've had Grace out of my head for awhile now. I heeded my sponsor when he advised me to forget about talking to her. Things have been going well in that regard. But that changed tonight. I was at the Eve of Eve, an annual party at the Tap House Pub. I don't go to the bar much, but once in awhile I drop in to see friends. Drinking in public isn't tempting for me. I prefer to socialize without alcohol. Long nights alone have been the test. I didn't expect Grace would be there. We don't have the same group of friends. I saw her walk in. I felt my stomach sink. I shrugged it off and went back to hanging out with the boys. Grace came up to chat with one of my buddies, a mutual friend. I decided I wanted to talk to her. I went up to her. I said a quick hello and thanks. She asked me why I was thanking her. I said that she had helped me realize the kind of person I had become. She said she had seen a *Facebook* photo of me drinking a beer. She was referring to a picture from Matt and Carla's engagement party. It was a Pepsi. I expected her doubt. I deserved doubt. I told her it was a Pepsi. I continued and told her only a fool would say they were an alcoholic as an excuse to get a girl back. She said it didn't matter—our relationship was too messed up; there was no point in talking about it. She said we could be friends. I asked how we could be friends, if we couldn't talk about the past. I said talking about it would help us both out. She said there were too many issues. She was right. I did mess up, bad. I wished her a Merry Christmas and went back to my buddies. My sponsor was right. I shouldn't have talked to her.

December 24 '08

I went to AA tonight, after hanging out with Mom and Dave for Christmas Eve at Mom's. At AA I told them what had happened the night before. After the meeting, my sponsor kindly didn't say I told you so. He told me that when the time comes, it will happen, but not if I try. He said if it doesn't, I have to accept the things I can't change. He told me I'm still early in recovery. I have to focus on myself. I'm back to focusing on myself. AA is a good reality check.

December 25 '08

My family is happy to see me happy in recovery. It sounds weird, but they're relieved I'm an alcoholic. It's the answer to their question about my past despair. They always knew something was blocking my happiness. For years, I made them feel they were walking on egg shells around me. I treated my brother like shit. I hated his views on life and thought he was a biased prick. I was the biased prick. I didn't care for him. He had always tried to have a healthy relationship with me, but I would shrug him off. We're building that relationship now, and we're good buddies. We've been battling each other on the tennis courts lately. He started the summer off with a couple of wins, but I'm starting to chalk up the W's. We both have become open-minded with each other's differences. He's a great guy. He's had my back since day one. I'm proud of his successes.

My Dad was over for Christmas morning—all four of us together for the first time in ages. Dad and Mom are friends now. Apparently, I had done some good during that mediating attempt. They were able to set up a meeting after a few back-and-forth discussions with me. I was able to convince them of each other's motives, and they met without grudges—the only way they could have fixed their problems with each other. It's nice to see them talking. I don't know how much progress has been made and how much was staged for our benefit, but I liked it. It was nice being together, laughing. They're all shocked at how healthy I've started to look.

My parents have both moved on. They're happy. I'm happy they're happy.

I got a Christmas bonus from work that wiped out my debt. I wasn't expecting a bonus. It never entered my thoughts. I'm in the pluses for the first time since the Kelowna casino blackout trip. It's a good feeling.

Merry Christmas!

December 26 '08

Tonight, after the meeting, I'm sitting down with my sponsor, at Tim Horton's, for a coffee. We are discussing my recovery. He asks how I am doing. I tell him things are slowly coming together. He tells me, "Luke, I think you are on the right track. You are ready to move onto Step Two. You have shown your commitment to AA with over thirty straight meetings. You are opening yourself up in AA and exposing your past life. I can say that I see lots of strength in you. What do you think? Do you feel you are ready to move on?"

"Please."

We chuckle. He knows the feeling.

I continue. "Step One has been easy to acknowledge, but hard to accept. Initially in AA, before my slip, I didn't think there was a chance in hell I was an alcoholic like the rest of you. But, in the back of my mind, I always knew I had a problem. And AA taught me that it's a lifelong problem that has no cure. Also, that it doesn't matter whether alcoholism is viewed as a disease or a self-inflicted addiction, because, in the end, I can't pick up that first drink, and that's all that matters. Through writing, I have come to realize I was powerless for years. And it got to the point that I didn't hit complete rock bottom, but, if I continued on the path I was on, I would soon have hit bottom hard. My life was becoming unmanageable. Near the end, I didn't give a shit about myself. I feel very lucky to have been given a second chance at life. And I will use it by taking one day at a time. I feel there is a lot left for me to fix. I made a lot of mistakes as an alcoholic. Listening to someone like you (who lost more than I did and has regained it all with time) gives me the strength to know the same can happen to me, too."

"And what about your ex? Have you come to understand you won't be with her again?"

"I haven't had that problem. I know it seems that way, because of how I talk about her. But I'm over us, as a couple. What I'm not over is how I treated her and the hurt and disappointment I caused. I know I can't be with her. I've accepted that. I just want her to see through my eyes, so she can see that it wasn't me that was a monster; it was the alcohol. That's all I want. I wish the best to her and her boyfriend. I think she would talk to me if she knew I didn't get sober as an excuse to be with her, and that I only want to talk to her to make amends."

"And that can happen. If it doesn't, you accept it. There are some things you can't change, and you have to accept that."

"I know." I pause. "And I know that I can never drink again. With alcohol, I'm destined for misery. Without alcohol, I'm destined for success. I won't fail."

"I've always liked your attitude, Luke. You have a lot of optimism. Are you ready to look at Step Two?"

"Sure am."

Step Two:

We came to believe that a Power greater than ourselves could restore us to sanity.

What can we believe in? AA does not demand belief; Twelve Steps are only suggestions. Importance of an open mind. Variety of ways to faith. Substitution of AA as higher power. Plight of the disillusioned. Roadblocks of indifference and prejudice. Lost faith found in AA. Problems of intellectuality and self-sufficiency. Negative and positive thinking. Self-righteousness. Defiance is an outstanding characteristic of alcoholics. Step Two is a rallying point to sanity. Right relation to God.

Twelve Steps and Twelve Traditions

December 27 '08

I'm off to Hawaii. Grace and I planned this trip half a year ago. Since it was my treat, I crossed her name off and put my buddy Andy's in her place. I don't know about this step. This trip will be perfect to help collect my thoughts. It'll be hard not to drink, since I've never spent a trip sober. I took vacations as an opportunity to drink throughout the day, as I would have no commitments for the day. I would be dumb not to drink all day. But I'm looking forward to get up at sunrise refreshed, go for a run, meditate, hit the beach, read, listen to my tunes, and chill. No thoughts of misery. No painful memories. No school, work, moving, or health to worry about. I love Hawaii. Paradise.

January 2 '09

I got my results from that extensive research paper I wrote on autism for my internship psychology program. I completed it when I was near my rock bottom. My advisor said my work showed tremendous growth in my professional development and that it was well researched and well written. That felt good. I also got my marks back for the term. I only took three classes. Another alcoholic mistake. After the internship psychology program, I was given nine credits. I didn't know they were non-diploma credits. I only registered for three classes then, thinking I needed seven courses to graduate, and I would take the other four the next term. I need ten. But it's for the better, since I was drunk for most of the term. I got Bs. I want As.

For my fourth-year psychology course, I wrote an extensive research paper on Alcoholics Anonymous. I did this through my early stages of recovery, then my slip, then official recovery. It was a term-long project. I told my teacher/advisor I had a friend in AA and wanted to learn more in order to help him out. After reading dozens of peer-reviewed articles, I came to realize AA is the best thing for me. It's the most successful grassroots self-help movement of our time. The two individuals who founded AA were a surgeon and a Wall Street stockbroker. Alcoholism affects millions. Anybody can be an alcoholic. We're not all bums. Many well-respected citizens suffer or have suffered from addiction. We're all human.

March 20 '09

Our flight was delayed a day and a half, so when I got back in early January I had to catch up on school. I wasn't able to get back into the swing of things with AA. I haven't had a drink. I've had a couple of urges, but, when I do, I read *Alcoholics Anonymous* or *Twelve Steps and Twelve Traditions*. I write, too. It's narrative therapy.

I wrote a note on *Facebook*, sharing my journey into recovery. After reading over this, I realized I had completed Step Two. This is what I wrote:

Step two has been a pain in my ass. It says I must be willing to believe in a power greater than myself that will restore me to sanity. It's been months, and I haven't been to AA, mainly because the combination of school, work, and the move into a new home became overwhelming. While I was attending AA regularly, I was sleeping like a baby. While writing this, I'm on my second unintentional all-nighter in a row. I had a three-hour nap yesterday. That's about it in the last fifty-plus hours. Insomnia is one of my triggers. I know I need AA, but I need to get past Step Two on my own before I go back and commit myself. An English essay did it for me. I finished it tonight/this morning, and I'm ready to go back. I could use some zzz's. I'm going to plagiarize my own work (if that's possible) and show you my conclusions. Remember, they're my thoughts. I'm not stating facts, just what I believe. If you're offended, it's because you're religious, and I apologize. In my defence, I have had religion preached to me throughout life, mostly from people I don't know, and it's time I spoke the truth instead of politely nodding. Here's the essay:

(Skip first paragraph) "I personally don't possess a vast knowledge regarding religion, which is why I chose this topic to research. As a recovering alcoholic, I have begun the Twelve Steps program through Alcoholics Anonymous. I reached Step Two a few months ago, the one regarding a faith in a higher power and found myself at a standstill. Religion, faith, and spirituality have come and gone throughout my life. I was born in a flexible Catholic family. Church attendance was not mandatory, but a belief in God was imposed. As a child struggling with a skin disease known as eczema (which, at the peak of severity, I was told by dermatologists from around North America that they hadn't seen a case worse than mine), I believed and looked up to God to help me combat my disease and find meaning within my life. Even though just walking and opening my eyes were a struggle, I never blamed God, because I knew positively that there was a purpose for my existence. However, instead of my life situation improving as the physical turmoil resided, it worsened. On paper, my life was filled with ambition—but my mind was still wrapped around my childhood. I was met with a sense of failure; I doubted God and His intentions. And then I met alcohol. I never believed in love at first taste, but it was fate. A substance you can buy in a store, with any ID, and the faster and more you drink the less you feel. Pure genius.

"Years went by, and the drinking progressed. As a practicing alcoholic, I brought God back into my life, hoping to find the solution to overcoming my personal burden. This started with a purchase of the Bible. Whilst reading the Bible, I became distraught regarding the word *holy* in the title. The stories depicted did not seem to portray holiness. I found myself struck with common logic reading the Ten Commandments. I didn't need to read "Thou shall not kill" to know I should not kill. I questioned the purpose of worshipping an invisible product. As a Catholic, I questioned my religion for believing in a talking snake. I didn't think I was creative enough to wrap my head around the understanding of a virgin birth. Did Jesus come from a stork? Which one is the fairy tale? Once again I threw away the notion of a creator known as God. I didn't become an atheist but an on-the-fence agnostic. My belief became: 'you can't prove to me there is a God, and you can't prove to me there isn't, so let's drop it.'

"Slowly digging my grave, with vodka by my side, I gave up believing in myself. And that's when it became a quick downward spiral. Self-doubt was drained with more drinking. More drinking turned into self-hatred. Self-hatred led to me giving up boxing, losing a close relationship, possibly eliminating myself from contention for graduate school, almost quitting my job, and putting myself in debt and on the brink of dropping out of school. The last one was my awakening. Near the end, not being able to hold off till I finished my school work, I started writing papers while drinking. When the papers were finished, so was I. Writing tests with a hangover couldn't have lasted much longer. Not to mention that my health was deteriorating.

"So, if I were to put God before myself, I could blame these problems on Him, right?"

(4 pages later) "Now that I have a better understanding of the obligations toward oneself and faith, let's look at my question posed

in the introduction: *If I were to put God before myself, could I blame my problems on Him?* The wording of the question is meant to be rhetorical to illustrate what nonsense it is. At my breaking point, I gave myself two options: take control of my life, trust myself, come clean, and get help; or give up, blame God (or whoever the hell else), and let life take its course. If I were to choose the latter, I wouldn't be writing this, because school wasn't part of the second option. Now that I have gained self-reliance for the first time in my life, I'm able to open my mind to faith and, with confidence, choose the necessary path to follow. And to begin that notion, I will quote Emerson, "who would be a man must be a nonconformist."

"I believe the idea of worship and the immoral acts committed throughout the Catholic system have given the name of God a bad taste. I believe those who hold God in faith individually, through spiritual grounds, will benefit through God's will. To be Protestant, Catholic, Jewish, or Muslim only divides society, separating fellowship. I believe it's plausible to accept the notion that beyond all matter, land, and body there may exist a creative intelligence, a spirit of the universe, and, ultimately, a power greater than myself—that will guide me morally and spiritually through my journey, helping me fulfill my obligations to society, through random acts of kindness and extensive education, to aid in solving society's imbalances, which *we* have created, not God. I believe earth was designed on the foundation of peace, love, harmony, and equality amongst mankind. But with imperialism, greed, religious diversity, and corruption we have created this world of destruction. Intelligence, open-mindedness, and acceptance of others can consolidate mankind. But to argue amongst one another to the point of nuclear threats will lead to nuclear warfare and ultimately the destruction of mankind. It looks like the answer is as simple as a commandment: Thou shall not discriminate against others' beliefs (unless they cause harm to others), nor shall you preach your own. Gain a sense of self-reliance, so you may help your fellow man. Create your identity through perseverance, confidence, and fellowship. This will spread the happy-face epidemic the universe desperately needs. Amen."

I know I preached anti-preaching. It's part of the program. I apologize. I'm not saying my belief is the only belief. As long as your belief system guides you morally and open-mindedly to the diversity of your fellow (wo)man, then knock yourself out.

Step Three:

Made a decision to turn our will and our lives over to the care of God <u>*as we understood Him.*</u>

Step Three is like the opening of a locked door. How shall we let God into our lives? Willingness is the key. Dependence as a means to independence. Dangers of self-sufficiency. Turning our will over to a higher power. Misuse of will power. Sustained and personal exertion necessary to conform to God's will.

Twelve Steps and Twelve Traditions

April 5 '09

Holy shit. It's not getting easier. As in Step Two, I'm met with doubt. I just gained self-reliance for the first time, and now I'm supposed to turn that over to God? I need to talk to my sponsor.

April 18 '09

I talked to my sponsor last week. I told him this step confuses me. I told him that I have now gained self-reliance, and I'm not ready to lose that. He said I'll always have my self-reliance. He said this step deals with letting go of control. Letting whoever or whatever my higher power is take over the control of my life. I asked him why I would want to do that. He said that in order for me to stop worrying about the world around me, and to focus on myself, I have to let go of control. He said we alcoholics are tight-asses, and we have a hard time with this one, because we've always sought control in our lives. He said this led us to the bottle. I told him I tend to be a hypochondriac, and I always worry about family, and that it would be nice to lose that sense of control. He said it'll relieve stress and help me focus on my life. I said it would be nice to stop worrying over stuff I know I have no control over for myself and others. He said to give it a shot. He said that whenever I feel a lack of control, I should talk to my higher power and tell it to take over. I said I would give it a shot.

April 23 '09

God and I had a long chat last night. I broke down. It was the night of my last final exam for the term. This is the time I used to get shitfaced in celebration. But, then again, I would drink the night before the exam, too. I spent the day in fear. I went to bed scared. I felt I had nothing to work toward anymore. Alcohol had been my motivation. Now I could only look forward to mornings, when I felt good, and reflect on those wasting the morning with a hangover. My friends pity me at night and envy me in the morning. I hate pity. I like that kind of envy. I went to bed. I said hi to God. I asked if handing over my control to Him was going to do any good. I said I would love to stop worrying about others. I said worrying for others had led to my self-destructive path. Tears filled my eyes. I said thank you. I made crying noises. I don't make crying noises. I said thank you for giving me a second chance. I told God I'm handing over my control to Him, because I trust He will guide me morally and spiritually. I told Him I have faith He will guide me through recovery and take care of the ones around me and the ones I've lost, whom He now entertains. I said thank you for having faith in me and not giving up on me. I wiped my tears. I said I knew this was all a lesson. I told Him I knew He had picked me for a reason, and I wouldn't let Him down. I told Him I would do lots of good with the lesson. I said thank you. I fell asleep in a minute. I had busted my ass studying for finals, so I could have a peaceful sleep. I had searched it. I found it. I love it.

Step Four:

Made a searching and fearless moral inventor of ourselves.

How instincts can exceed their proper function. Step Four is an effort to discover our liabilities. Basic problem of extremes in instinctive drives. Misguided moral inventory can result in guilt, grandiosity, or blaming others. Assets can be noted in liabilities. Self-justification is dangerous. Willingness to take inventory brings light and new confidence. Step Four is the beginning of lifetime practice. Common symptoms of emotional insecurity are worry, anger, self-pity, and depression. Inventory reviews relationships. Importance of thoroughness.

Twelve Steps and Twelve Traditions

April 25 '09

This book is my moral inventory. I left two things out. Betraying a friend and fights.

Step Five:

Admitted to God, to ourselves, and to another human being the exact nature of our wrongs.

Twelve steps deflate ego. Step Five is difficult but necessary to sobriety and peace of mind. Confession is an ancient discipline. Without fearless admission of defects, few could stay sober. What do we receive from Step Five? Beginning of true kinship with man and God. Loss of sense of isolation. Receive forgiveness, and give it; learn humility, honesty, and realism about ourselves. Complete honesty needed. Danger of rationalization. How to choose the person in whom to confide. Results are tranquility and consciousness of God. Oneness with God and man prepares us for the following step.

Twelve Steps and Twelve Traditions

April 25 '09

This step will be good for me. I've had a couple of close friends and Aunt Danielle read the rough manuscript which means I've admitted a complete confession of the nature of my wrongs to them. Lots of people know about my betrayal to my friend. I'll have to find someone close to tell about my fights. There's not much to the fights. It's the least of my past. But street fighting isn't cool.

June 25 '09

Step Five is complete. After I'd completed my spring school courses (making up for those credits), Mom invited me to Hawaii with her, my little cousin Danielle, Mom's friend Marianne, and her daughter Jessica. One night, when the young girls were out exploring the island, I sat down with the ladies, Mom and Marianne. They were talking about funny moments of the old days when they were stewardesses together for Wardair. We laughed. The conversation started getting serious. Marianne reflected on a memory and started talking about defending friends. A light bulb went off in my head. I waited for a silent moment. I eased into the conversation.

"I think its okay to fight, if you're defending a friend. What do you think?" I look at them both. Marianne is thinking of her answer, Mom knowing me pretty well, looks at me curiously.

"Do you have something on your mind, Luke?"

I prepare for Step Five.

"Well … you know … street fights are dumb, but when a friend's at risk, I think it's appropriate to kick some butt." I pause. I smile.

They laugh.

"Go on, Luke."

I pause. I think about how to tell Mom and Marianne, who I just met, about my fights.

"All right, all right. I have some things I have to spill." I look at Mom. I think of how to start. "Mom, I've been in a couple more fights than I've told you about. Nothing serious. Just a couple of scratches." I don't give them time to put in their two cents. I decide to start with the minor one. I continue. "One time, at a bar on Whyte, I didn't end up fighting, just defended a buddy. My buddy accidently knocked this drink out of this preppy boy's hand. My buddy apologized. The other guy, collar up, looking sweet, acting tough, grabbed my buddy's shirt. I was a few feet away and I instantly ran up to them, pushed my buddy aside, grabbed the guy's dress shirt with my left hand, and had my right ready to land one—but within a second a bouncer grabbed my fist, put me in a hold, and kicked me out. So no harm done on that one." I breathe.

I start again, softly. "All right, next. In a bar on Jasper Avenue, this guy was making fun of my buddy. My buddy told me about it, just for conversation's sake, since he wasn't a fighter. I asked who it was. He showed me. Drunk with power, and dumb as a doorknob, I decided to take care of it. I told the guy to meet me outside. He ended up coming out with his steroid buddy. When I saw this guy, I laughed. I knew this wasn't going to be good. I could barely stand on my own. He knocked me out. My buddies rushed outside to break it up. I got up, ripped shirt, cut lip, and started laughing. I specifically remember laughing, because it showed me how much I had stopped caring about myself." I breathe.

"Okay, two down. In Montreal, Sergio, my old roommate from boarding school, and I got in a fight at a McGill University party. A couple of friends from home had come out to visit me, Brad, Jill, and Jill's friend. Serge had a crush on my friend Jill. This guy at the party had one, too. Serge got jealous, said some smart-assed comment to this six-foot-four, lanky guy. The guy said something back. Serge, the tempered rugby player, got a little mad. I told Serge to take a walk. He did. I told the guy to cool it; we're all here for a good time. I said, 'I don't know you, and my friend Jill looks uncomfortable with this situation, so you might as well go.' As I was turning away, he sucker-punched me."

"What's *sucker punch* mean?" Mom ruins my consistency. Being my mother, she should know this.

I smile and shake my head. "Lucie, Lucie, a sucker punch is when someone punches you without you being aware it's coming. A fight is usually initiated before punches are thrown. Anyhow, after he punched me, my face turned to the right, I looked down, saw the plastic cup of beer in my hand, tossed it in his face, and charged him. I gave him a couple of shots, then, within seconds, Serge came bolting in, tackled the guy, and started pounding him. After he got a few shots, I grabbed Serge and said, 'Let's get out of here.' We went outside and started celebrating our first fight together. We had always wanted to do that; we had talked about it at school, ha ha. It was really just a joke, though."

They grimace.

I continue.

"So we went back into the building. Walking up the stairs, we saw the guy we had fought, blood coming out of his nose, and a cut by his eye. His hands were held behind his back by the security guards. We acted casual. The guy snapped, saying, 'It's those fuckers! They did this! They started the fucking fight! Let me go, you pigs!' Knowing how far he had dug his hole with that comment and being the smart-ass I am, I piped up, 'We just got here. This guy is loaded. Book him, boys.' Serge and I started laughing and walked back into the party. That fight was funny, but karma probably didn't think so. I ended up walking back to my apartment for an hour and a half with the hiccups."

The ladies laugh. Marianne laughs more than Mom. Mom seems iffy on the subject.

"So, *son*, any other fights you want to share with your mother?"

"You betcha. I think this is the last one. When living downtown, I was at this bar with a bunch of friends. Dave and his buddies were there, too. At one point in the night, a few friends and I were sitting at a booth. A friend of mine came up to the booth. She told me that this guy was creeping her out and wanted to know if I would dance with her, so he would back off. I said I would love to dance with her. Once on the dance floor, I could tell who the guy was. He was standing in the corner staring at us. I glared at him as to say, 'Don't touch my girl,' then ignored him. A song later, the guy came up to us. He said some smart-assed comment to me. Again, drunk with power and dumb as a doorknob, I responded, saying something back. I went back to dancing. He sucker-punched me. I have to learn not to say something and then turn away."

Marianne laughs, Mom nods, as if she's cool knowing what sucker punch means.

"Instinctively, I went toward him. A guy on the dance floor who saw the punch grabbed me and told me not to bother. I nodded and agreed. I turned to see my friend looking shocked and scared. She looked hurt. I told her I'd be right back. I walked off the dance floor, with the guy in my peripheral vision. I walked around the dance floor, saw a couple of buddies, tapped one on the shoulder, told him to have my back, and kept walking. The guy was standing with his back to me, talking to a few friends. I tapped him on the shoulder. He turned. I grabbed his shirt, said 'Fuck you,' and started punching him. I got a couple of shots in, then, out of nowhere—*boom*—I'm on the ground in the turtle position, getting kicked to the body and head by four or more feet. Turned out some guy had beer-bottled me in the head from behind. Within seconds, I got choked by a bouncer, who tossed me out the bar by the back doors. The other few guys got kicked out the front doors.

"A couple of buddies, who are big and known for not losing fights, saw what had happened. They followed the guys out the front doors. The two of them beat up four guys. They were twice their size though, so it evens it out. As for me, I had a mild concussion. Dave had heard what had happened; he called and told me to call him when I got home. A half hour later he called me, asking where the hell I was, since I only lived five minutes away. I looked up at the street sign and realized I had walked the wrong way. I told Dave; he called me a dipshit and said it was serious I got home safe and not jumped. I ended up home fine, though. Walking back, I noticed people looking at me funny. When I got home, I realized it was because the right side of my face was covered in dry blood. Ha ha—oops. The only marks I got from that fight were a cut on the head from the bottle and a couple of minor bruises from the kicks."

Mom looks disgusted.

Marianne looks interested.

I'm relieved it's over.

"Well, thanks for that, ladies. Have yourselves a great night. I have some writing to do. You just helped me complete Step Five."

They give me funny looks.

"Ah ha, so that's what just happened," Mom says. Relieved there was a purpose.

"Yeah, I wouldn't do that for fun. I'm not proud of street fighting. It's dumb. But they're a part of my past. Pretty harmless stories, though. Goodnight, Marianne. Goodnight, Mom." I kiss Mom on both cheeks.

"Goodnight, Luke. Great chat," Marianne chuckles.

"Goodnight, son." Mom says smiling at Marianne.

Time for another peaceful sleep.

Step Six:

Were entirely ready to have God remove all these defects of character.
Step Six is necessary to spiritual growth. The beginning of a lifetime job. Recognition of difference between striving for objective—and perfection. Why we must keep trying. "Being ready" is all-important. Taking action is necessary. Delay is dangerous. Rebellion may be fatal. Point at which we abandon limited objectives and move toward God's will for us.
Twelve Steps and Twelve Traditions

July 6 '09

I've come to believe in a higher power. My higher power is named God. Not the religious God. Not the God from any Bible. My God. Not based on science, but faith. My spiritual Lord. My individual creative intelligence that guides me with strength and support. Someone to talk to. I don't ask for anything. My prayer is conversation. I talk about what's making me happy and what's making me distraught. And if there is something blocking my happiness, I talk to God about how I'm going to fix that. Each time, I thank God for keeping me around. I ask God each time to entertain my loved ones whose souls live on. I say thanks for another twenty-four hours of sobriety. If I'm frustrated before our talk, I speak till I feel hope. Life is complex, but it can be made simple. I keep simplicity in my complex life.

As for asking to remove my defects of character, I've done that with His guidance. I don't have to tell Him what I did. He knows. I spoke to Him about my defects being removed, as long as I keep doing what I'm doing, He has my back. He didn't say anything, but I understand His silence. I'm on the right path.

Step Seven:

Humbly asked Him to remove our shortcomings.
What is humility? What can it mean to us? The avenue to true freedom of the human spirit. Necessary aid to survival. Value of ego-puncturing. Failure and misery transformed by humility. Strength from weakness. Pain is the admission price to new life. Self-centered fear chief activator of defects. Step Seven is change in attitude, which permits us to move out of ourselves toward God.
Twelve Steps and Twelve Traditions

July 11 '09

I've become humble with myself. Asking Him to remove this is not what I do. Action and time have done so. His guidance was key.
I'm still a smart-ass. But, it's all in fun.

Step Eight:

Made a list of all persons we had harmed, and became willing to make amends to them all.

This step and the next two are concerned with personal relations. Learning to live with others is a fascinating adventure. Obstacles: reluctance to forgive; non-admission of wrongs to others; purposeful forgetting. Necessity of exhaustive survey of past. Deepening insight results from thoroughness. Kinds of harm done to others. Avoiding extreme judgments. Taking the objective view. Step Eight is the beginning of the end of isolation.

Twelve Steps and Twelve Traditions

Mom and Dad: deceit, lies, attitude.

Dave: not allowing him to build a relationship with me, attitude, deceit, lies.

Grace: deceit, lies, hurt, doubt, jealousy, insecurity, sadness.

Tommy: difficulty, attitude, being a shithead.

Funk: betrayal. His girlfriend kissed me. I could have prevented it.

Girl I called just another slut and the drunkest girl in St. Albert.

Myself: I caused more harm to myself than anyone else.

Step Nine:

Made direct amends to such people wherever possible, except when to do so would injure them or others.

A tranquil mind is the first requisite for good judgment. Good timing is important in making amends. What is courage? Prudence means taking calculated chances. Amends begins when we join AA. Peace of mind cannot be bought at the expense of others. Need for discretion. Readiness to take consequences of our past and to take responsibility for well-being of others is spirit of Step Nine.

Twelve Steps and Twelve Traditions

July 12 '09

I apologized to the girl. I told her I hadn't forgiven myself for saying some of the things I had said to her and that I should have treated her well. I told her she was a good person, and good people deserve to be treated with respect and kindness. She accepted my apology and said it had been long forgotten and that she's happy for me taking that step in my life to better myself. She's a good person.

July 13 '09

Mom turned fifty-four today. I mean thirty-five. Well, she looks thirty-five. Dave and I took Mom to this great Thai restaurant, called Kai, on Jasper Avenue. While we were eating, I figured it was time.

I tell them I'm on Step Nine. I look at Dave. He shrugs his shoulders, as if to say I have nothing to apologize for. Getting that impression from his body language, I laugh out loud. "Give me a break." This is code for, "Shut the hell up. You've been waiting for this, asshole."

Dave laughs.

"You're right; start apologizing. This better be good."

I look him in the eyes and show real sincerity.

"Sorry for being a jerk to you all these years."

He shrugs, as if to say I shouldn't be hard on myself.

I nod, to say it's true.

He nods with a slight grin in agreement.

I continue. "Sorry for not letting you build that relationship you have always tried to have with me."

Dave's appreciative. Mom's eyes well up.

I continue, "Thank you for never giving up that relationship. Thanks for having my back, since I was born, when you offered Mom a diaper when her water broke."

We laugh.

"Thanks for sticking by my side all these years and never giving up on me. It means a lot to me."

We give each other a handshake.

"Thanks, Puke. I appreciate your apology. I forgive you. Not only do I forgive you, but I'm very proud and amazed at what you're doing. It's great to have you back, bro."

Next. I look at Mom. I ease into it.

"Mom, sorry for all the money I wasted." We laugh. I get serious. "Sorry for hiding my past life. I only did it to protect you from hurting over my burden. Sorry I wasn't the son you thought I was."

"Son, you have always been everything I could want in a son, if not more." Tears make waves in her eyes.

"You're sappy, but sweet. Mom, I'm sorry I let you down. Don't say anything. I know you think I haven't, but I've looked at it from every angle. I could have been there for you more. I would have talked to you more during that tough time. I could and would have done a lot more to make up for all you have done for me, but I couldn't take care of myself." Mom understands—she's a recovering alcoholic as well. "I love you and thank you for always being so bright and hopeful. You gave me my strength."

Mom hugs me.

"I accept your apology. I'm so proud of you, Lukie."

"Thanks, Mom. I'm still working on pride. I'm proud of you." I pick up my delicious Pepsi and raise it up. "To the lady who looks more beautiful with age. We love you, Mom."

Dave picks up his frosty glass of water. "Love you, Mom."

Mom picks up her ice-cold Diet Pepsi with lime. A tear is on her cheek. "I love you boys."

July 20 '09

I've been sober for eight months. Grace and I have been broken up for a year. It took me a week to build the strength to call her. I called. She didn't answer, which I expected. I messaged her, saying I had reached Step Nine of the Twelve Steps program of Alcoholics Anonymous and was wondering if we could talk. She didn't reply, which I expected. I've accepted the "Things I Cannot Change." The things I cannot change are making amends and having her forgive me. Next.

July 22 '09

I went to Dad's for dinner tonight. While eating our steaks, we watched *Two and a Half Men*. I joked to Dad that I'd have no problem being an alcoholic if I could live the role Charley Sheen plays on the show. We laughed. While we were on the topic of alcoholism, I told Dad about trying to get hold of my ex. He told me to forget about it. I told him the Serenity Prayer suggested I should, too. I then continued on to Step Nine.

"Dad, I want to apologize for my deceitful past. I'm sorry for keeping my drinking from you. I'm sorry I kept my true identity from my own Dad."

He nods.

I continue.

"There's something I haven't told you, but I'm guessing you have an idea. In boarding school, I could have been expelled from the school on numerous occasions, which would have wasted your money and my future."

Dad's eyes widen.

"You did what? You were drinking heavy then, too?"

"I was just getting started at that point. If it helps, I was told by a few people that I drank the most they had seen without ever getting busted once."

"I would have killed you." Dad keeps a straight face.

"I know you would have. And I always had that in the back of my mind, but it didn't stop me. The addiction was too powerful."

"Do you know how many extra hours I worked to put you through that school—the cars I bought, fixed, and sold?" Dad glares at me, then smiles. "You're lucky, Luke."

"Don't I know it. But, hey, I'd make a great con artist."

We laugh.

"Thanks for always being there for me, Dad. For being the male role model that I've admired all my life. Thanks for doing everything in your power to make sure I can pursue my dreams. Thanks, Pops."

"I'm proud of you, son. But I would have killed you." He smiles. "I love you, Luke."

"I love you too, old man."

August 2 '09

Tommy came by today. We haven't hung out for awhile, so he came over to catch up. We were playing Wii Tennis, when I decided it was time for my apology to him.

I look at Tommy after another match win (I don't lose at Wii Tennis. I became a pro while recovering in Mom's basement. It's been fifty-plus straight match wins). I nod.

"What?" he asks, waiting for a smart-ass reply.

"I'm pretty awesome. You can call me Kid Clutch." I make up nicknames for myself.

"For the last time, Luke, you can't make up your own nicknames!"

I nod again.

"Another thing."

Annoyed, Tommy replies, "What?"

"Sorry for being an annoying, bitter prick the last couple of years. You dealt with more of my shit than most of the guys, and I thank you for sticking by."

"You're still annoying. But I always got your back, bro."

I nod again.

"Thanks, Tom Boy. Right back attcha."

Tommy nods back.

Somehow, Tommy built some momentum and took two straight sets. But don't worry; Kid Clutch took the match three sets to two. The streak stays alive, and my conscience eases with time.

August 4 '09

Tyler and I haven't been able to coordinate a time to meet for coffee. He called me tonight, while I was parking at the baseball diamond and getting my gear ready to play some ball. I figured the phone was my best opportunity. Tyler was asking what I was up to. I told him and asked the same. When he finished, I began my apology.

"Funk, the reason I've wanted to get together one on one was so I could apologize, again, but this time sober. I know I've apologized in the past. And I know you were pissed at me for a year. You forgave me that night at the bar, after you punched me in the nuts and said we were cool, but I still haven't forgiven myself. I know I didn't initiate the kiss, but if I'd been sober I could have prevented it. You've been one of my closest friends since I can remember, and I can't believe I had put myself in that situation. It was implanted in my head for months. I couldn't shake it off, man. I felt awful."

"Well, like you said, Luke, I have forgiven you. It obviously pissed me off, and, to be honest, it gave me trust issues for awhile after that."

"I bet it did. The only reason I made sure you found out it happened was so you would know what was going on in your relationship. But you have a great girl, now, don't you?"

"Yeah, man."

"That's good. I'm happy for you."

"Thanks. And, as before, I accept your apology."

"Thanks Funkmasterflex. We'll have to get together soon, when I'm out of school. I graduate in a week."

"For sure, dude. Good luck at ball."

"Thanks. Have a good night, Funk."

August 4 '09

After ball, I came home, did some homework, and now I'm writing. I've finished my apologies to others. It's time for my own apology.

Sorry for becoming everything you hated. Sorry for hurting you. Sorry for letting you hurt others. Sorry for letting your addiction control your thoughts. Sorry it took over your life, soul, and heart. Sorry it broke you down. You're lucky you're alive. You're lucky for what you have. You're lucky you have a strong support group. You're lucky you got a second chance. Thank you for never giving up on yourself. Thank you for being strong during your weakest hour. Thank you for spreading the word about isolated addictions and trying to make a difference. Thank you for admitting defeat—I know how stubborn you are. Thanks for staying true to yourself.

That was confusing. Anyhow, this step has completed my personal recovery. The rest are for everyday life. I am at peace.

Step Ten:

Continued to take personal inventory and when we were wrong promptly admitted it.

Can we stay sober and keep emotional balance under all conditions? Self-searching becomes a regular habit. Admit, accept, and patiently correct defects. Emotional hangover. When past is settled with, present challenges can be met. Varieties of inventory. Anger, resentment, jealousy, envy, self-pity, hurt pride—these all led to the bottle. Self-restraint is the first objective. Insurance against "big shot-ism." Let's look at credits as well as debits. Examination of motives.

Twelve Steps and Twelve Traditions

This step applies to every day. I use this step to the best of my ability. I don't hold grudges anymore. If I don't agree with something or other that someone says to me, I speak my mind immediately and inform the person that what they're saying isn't cool with me. I used to bottle shit up. That caused stress, which caused stomach problems, and which can cause other health problems. Now I say what I have to say, and I always end the debate with whomever it is on good terms. Grudges are a waste of time. Lots of times grudges begin from miscommunication. Life's too short to pollute the mind with useless garbage. I'm not dating, so I don't have jealousy. When I do start dating, I don't expect to be jealous. I'm confident in myself, and I know alcohol caused my jealousy in the past. Self-pity is long gone. I've always hated the word pity. I'm happy with my life. That's self-pride. When I'm wrong, I'm capable of admitting it—if I'm completely sure I'm wrong, that is. I'm able to man up and take responsibility for my own actions and never blame issues in my mind on others. This step keeps the mind's air clean.

Step Eleven:

Sought through prayer and meditation to improve our conscious contact with God, as we understood Him, *praying only for knowledge of His will for us and the power to carry that out.*

Meditation and prayer the main channels to higher power. Connection between self-examination and meditation and prayer. An unshakable foundation for life. How shall we meditate? Meditation has no boundaries. An individual adventure. First result is emotional balance. What about prayer? Daily petitions for understanding God's will and grace to carry it out. Actual results of prayer are beyond question. Rewards of meditation and prayer.

Twelve Steps and Twelve Traditions

I've been looking forward to this step since the first day of AA, when it was read aloud. I felt relief finally finding a step I liked. Well, the meditation part. A few years ago, I took a weekend course on the art of meditation. I went to this seminar in hope of clearing my mind to cure my insomnia; then, I'd be able to stop medicating myself with alcohol to fall asleep. Another self-help attempt. Naturally, this didn't work, since I was hungover every time I meditated. It didn't stop me from drinking, but I was able to reach that outer spirituality a couple of times for short periods. Throughout my sobriety, I've meditated off and on; now it's time to get a daily rhythm going.

Step Twelve:

Having had a spiritual awakening as a result of these steps, we tried to carry this message to alcoholics, and to practice these principles in all our affairs.

Joy of living is the theme of the twelfth step. *Action* is its keyword. Giving that asks no reward. Love that has no price tag. What is spiritual awakening? A new state of consciousness and being is received as a free gift. Readiness to receive the gift lies in practice of Twelve Steps. The magnificent reality. Rewards of helping other alcoholics. Kinds of Twelve Step work. Problems of Twelve Step work. What about the practice of these principles in *all* our affairs? Monotony, pain, and calamity turned to good use by practice of steps. Difficulties of practice. "Two-stepping." Switch to "twelve-stepping" and demonstrations of faith. Growing spiritually is the answer to our problems. Placing spiritual growth first. Domination and overdependence. Putting our lives on a give-and-take basis. Dependence upon God is necessary to recovery of alcoholics. "Practicing these principles in *all* our affairs": Domestic relations in AA. Outlook upon material matters changes. So do feelings about personal importance. Instincts restored to true purpose. Understanding is key to right attitudes, right action key to good living.

Twelve Steps and Twelve Traditions

I don't believe in seeing God or some form of hallucination. I've never hallucinated and don't plan on it ever happening. My spiritual awakening is waking up refreshed and excited for the day—not with a hangover. My spiritual awakening is finding real happiness from life's little things: visiting Grandpa Dick; seeing my parents and brother; playing tennis three or four times a week with my bro or buddies Hoops and Chris; playing slo-pitch beer league baseball with my close buddies, getting our asses kicked (it's our first year);

kicking my buddies' asses at basketball; tossing around the football; living close to my buddies; hanging out with my buddies. Having confessed to a mom from work that I'm a recovering alcoholic and that I worked with her son for over a year on a hangover—and having the mom say she's proud of me for taking care of it, and that they never noticed, and it never affected my job, so it's no big deal—is an awakening of confidence. Knowing what I was doing as a job, and telling people that I drank every night before working with autistic kids, made me hold back from telling people. I knew I was good at my job and exposing this would only stigmatize me. But that's not the case, because I still managed to excel at my job on seventy-percent capability. Having acceptance for my past life is *the* spiritual awakening. Being happy and finding true happiness without hooch in my life is a spiritual awakening. I hated life and each day it provided, and it was because of one readymade store-bought substance that I thought I could never live without. My spiritual awakening is finding faith in recovery and sobriety.

Sobriety and recovery are two different subjects. Two-thirds of those who get sober will relapse. The ones who stay sober are the ones who are fulfilled from sobriety. The ones who are fulfilled from sobriety are the ones who follow the recovery process with an open mind. Unfortunately, many people who get sober become more depressed. They aren't recovering alcoholics; they are struggling alcoholics, who still have courage to fight their addiction with the hopes of recovery. Recovery consists of following the Twelve Steps, keeping contact with AA as much as needed (preferably consistently at the beginning of recovery), keeping active, building meaningful relationships, looking at what is had and not what is lost, taking one day at a time, not listening to the devil whispering in your ear to take a sip (it goes away later in recovery), and, ultimately, enjoying life without alcohol.

I was never aware of the consequences of my actions. I was fifteen. I didn't know the implications of my behaviours. I drank to rid the pain. I thought it was temporary. I didn't know I could become addicted to alcohol. I was oblivious of my fate. It wasn't until I went to university to study psychology that I knew what alcoholism truly meant. At this point, I was already an addict. I studied alcoholism in many different psychology and sociology courses. I drank while I read about broken lives. I couldn't stop. I was already a statistic before I found out I was one. I wish I was aware. I wish I knew what could have happened. But I didn't. And I'm okay with that, because now you know.

If it's too late and you are where I was, AA is a free ticket to freedom. It's up to you to take that first step. Character is built during your weakest hour. Find the strength and persevere.

Official Date of Sobriety: November 20 '08

****

Thank you, Mom and Dad; you two have given me life throughout life. You have given me everything I've needed to be who I am and to become who I want to be. You two are my biggest gifts—thank you. Thank you, Dave. I look up to you, big bro. Thank you, Aunt Danielle, for helping me with this book and for all your support throughout my life. There's a reason I came to you for help. I trust you. Thank you, Grandpa; you're my hero. Thank you, Matt; you've always had my back. Thank you, Tommy; you never gave up on a shithead. Thank you, Grace; you stuck around long enough for me to see what I had become. You're beautiful. Thank you, Dr. Handman. You did everything you could; you're a good doctor. Thank you, AA; you welcomed me at my weakest hour and showed me the path to success. A big thanks to the families I worked with—who supported and backed me up during a dark time of lies and manipulations from my former employer after she heard about my past. Your acceptance and faith in me have meant the world to me. Thank you so much. Thank you, Uncle Gary—thank you for my second chance. You woke me up before it was too late. Thank you, stranger, for reading my book. Thank you for being open minded toward my life. Alcoholics thank you for accepting us and forgiving our pasts. Peace and Love.